With a broad range of useful illustrations and candid self disclosures, Charles Cerling identifies the conditioned responses to need which trigger in us all those persistent failures we call "bad habits". Along with biblical counsel for the cleansing of these "besetting sins," Cerling provides positive steps for dismantling and effectively reversing these defeating practices. Assignments closing each chapter provide a counter process aimed at breaking the chain of habitual response, setting us free to establish a positive Christian self-image.

Dwight Hervey Small
Professor Emeritus of Sociology
Westmont College;
Author: *Your Marriage Is God's Affair*
            and *How Should I Love You*

Freedom From Bad HABITS

Charles Cerling, Jr.

Here's Life Publishers

FREEDOM FROM BAD HABITS
by Charles Cerling, Jr.

Published by
HERE'S LIFE PUBLISHERS, INC.
P. O. Box 1576
San Bernardino, CA 92402

Library of Congress Catalog Card 84-062384
ISBN 0-89840-079-1
HLP Product No. 950832

© 1984, Here's Life Publishers, Inc.
All rights reserved.

Printed in the United States of America.
Unless otherwise indicated, all Scripture quotations are taken from the Living Bible, © 1971 by Tyndale House Publishers, Wheaton, Illinois, and are used by permission.

FOR MORE INFORMATION, WRITE:

L.I.F.E.—P.O. Box A399, Sidney South 2000, Australia
Campus Crusade for Christ of Canada—Box 300, Vancouver, B.C., Canada V6C 2x3
Campus Crusade for Christ—103 Frair Street, Reading RGI IEP, Berkshire, England
Lay Institute for Evangelism—P.O. Box 8786, Auckland ³, New Zealand
Great Commission Movement of Nigeria, P.O. Box 500, Jos, Plateau State Nigeria, West Africa
Life Ministry—P.O. BoxÇBus 91015, Auckland Park 2006, Republic of South Africa
Campus Crusade for Christ International—Arrowhead Springs, San Bernardino, CA 92414, U.S.A.

Dedicated to Dwight Small for

his years of encouragement in

my writing endeavors.

Contents

1

Frustration and Relief

Do you have a habit you wish you could overcome? Probably. If not, you wouldn't have picked up this book.

Most of us have at least one habit we wish we could break. In fact, if people inquired closely, they would likely discover you are discouraged because you haven't been able to break some bad habit. On numerous occasions you've tried, but you can't seem to make it. You may even have given up. You've tried and failed so often that you're convinced your habit will go with you to the grave. So you no longer try.

When this is the case, however, your guilt prevents you from becoming all God wants you to be. You may not be conscious of your guilt, but Satan will use it at key moments. He'll whisper in your ear, "How can you witness when you [insert your habit]?" And you quickly back off for fear of being hypocritical. The author of Hebrews said in 12:1, "Let us strip off anything that slows us down or holds us back, and especially those sins that wrap themselves so tightly around our feet and trip us up; and let us run with patience the particular race that God has set before us." These habits are weights that hold you back from effective Christian living and ministry.

If that description is true of you, I have good news. There is no need for a bad habit to hold you back. In fact, there is more support now for throwing off the habits that bind us than ever before.

During the past decade, psychologists have studied the growing drug problem, alcoholism, and overeating, as well as lesser habits such as fingernail biting and hair twisting. These studies have uncovered basic principles for breaking any bad habit; so you can now combine them with the insights of the Bible to break yourself free from the habits that bind you.

As a teenager I struggled long and hard with unclean thoughts, a habit that sapped my desire to continue living as a Christian. Although I might win for a few days, it took such effort that I would be drained. Then I would fail again and kick myself around for the next few days for my failure.

At that time I was working with a well-known Christian counselor who had a ministry to thousands. I discussed my problem with him and asked for his advice. He gave me counsel derived from the Bible that he felt was based on key principles for breaking a bad habit. However, he applied those principles in such a way that he violated some basic truths of habit breaking recently discovered by psychologists. I followed his advice. But because he didn't understand the principles of psychology, he created more problems for me than he solved. In the end, I failed even worse than before. I was ready to quit.

Then I turned to a Christian psychologist on the campus of my school. He gave me different advice about how to break my habit. His counsel didn't sound very spiritual, because he made no reference to the Bible. But what he said was very biblical. It was also psychologically informed. In a few days my habit was gone. I occasionally struggled with it in the future, but each time, as I applied the principles he gave me, I succeeded in overcoming the habit again.

I have since learned that under the Spirit's direction, we can combine both biblical teaching and psychological principles in our fight to conquer bad habits. Since I began college, I have sought to integrate psychology and Christian teaching, but many schools have resisted this. I have been told again and again by well-meaning professors that you have to study either the Bible or psychology — you can't work on both at the same time. On the other hand, minister friends have described counseling problems in which they have applied the Bible without related insights from psychology, and I have listened in horror to their advice as I've realized it created more problems than it solved.

I'm convinced the Bible has the answers to life's problems, but I also think that when it is misapplied it creates problems. When a person seeks God's will, he should begin with the Bible.

But it is foolish to ignore the related insights of psychology. For a while, I turned away from Christian writing on human problems because I felt it was simplistic and poorly done. But I was not comfortable with this. Then I found that people like Norman Wright, Bruce Narramore, and Dwight Small were doing a good job using both Christian teaching and contemporary psychology. I also discovered Larry Crabb, who gives a philosophical base for integrating psychology and Christian thought. He calls his method "spoiling the Egyptians," relating it to Israel's taking the best of Egypt when they left for the promised land. What he means is that without giving up our Christian principles, we should integrate the best of secular psychology with Christian teaching. As I attempted to apply the methods of these people to the problem of habits, I found that either one without the other is inadequate.

Christian teaching that does not also contain key insights into human behavior can be applied in a way that creates rather than solves problems, as happened to me. On the other hand, secular psychology, with its implicit rejection of God, gives a person no power to change, particularly in dealing with the effects of sin. As a result, I have attempted to integrate the best of both worlds to help people break the habits that bind them. I now think you, too, can be free of any habit that is bothering you.

I'm not going to say it will be easy. Nothing worth having comes easily. It will take work. It will mean perseverance. But if you stick with the plan I give in this book, you should be able to break any habit you have.

In making such strong statements, I begin with some basic assumptions. First, I assume you have committed your life to Jesus Christ and therefore have the Holy Spirit inside you to provide the motivation and power you will need to overcome your habit. I also assume you are more than just a Christian. I assume you are a person who wants to follow Jesus Christ wherever He leads you. You are committed to Him throughout each aspect of your living. If such is not the case, I urge you to obtain the two booklets listed at the end of this chapter. From them you can learn both how to accept Christ as Savior and how to be filled with the Holy Spirit as a regular part of your Christian experience.

Now let me show how you can most effectively use this book. Begin by reading it from cover to cover *without attempting to do anything about your habit*. You need to get the big picture before you start working on the details. Habits are far larger than most people think. Even simple habits usually have much more to them than you might imagine. So read the whole book before working on the assigned tasks. While reading, ask the Holy Spirit to help you see what you need to learn to break your habit.

Then prayerfully work through it again, one task at a time. Each chapter contains a single key idea, principle, or project essential in breaking your habit. Take them slowly, spending a few days to a week on each one as you seek the Holy Spirit's power to control your habit. If you follow each step in dependence on Him, you'll win the battle with your habit. This book is a manual with regular assignments for each step.

To make your battle plan even more effective, work through this book with a Christian friend. We need our friends when we're working on a bad habit. We need their support when we feel down. We need their assistance in seeing things we might overlook. We need their encouragement to continue when we feel like quitting. This is true even though your habit might be one that embarrasses you. A friend often means the difference between success and failure. Solomon said, "Two can accomplish more than twice as much as one, for the results can be much better. If one falls, the other pulls him up; but if a man falls when he is alone, he's in trouble" (Eccl. 4:9-10).

This principle can be taken even further. If you're working to correct a habit that you can discuss in a group, get together with a few friends and work on your habits together. There's nothing quite like the camaraderie and support that comes from tackling a problem together to give you the incentive to persist. Paul said in Galatians 6:2, "Share each other's troubles and problems, and so obey our Lord's command." A support group will enable you to stick with it even when you're discouraged. So get with some friends and work on overcoming your habits together. In the end, you'll all benefit.

A final note. As you get into this book, you'll see that I call some things habits that you might not. Psychologists see habits more broadly than other people. They see most of life as composed of habits. They classify such different things as fingernail biting, drug addiction, overeating, talkativeness, procrastination, house-cleaning style, and much more as habits. Be aware of this broader usage as you read.

Further reading:

Have You Heard of the Four Spiritual Laws? and *Have You Made the Wonderful Discovery of the Spirit-filled Life?*, booklets published by Here's Life Publishers, San Bernardino, California. © Campus Crusade for Christ, Inc., 1965 and 1966.

2

Habits Are Valuable

Just before Joyce took her first practice roll, I asked, "Which foot do you lead with when you bowl?"

As was their custom, Joyce and Sam Moulds had arrived early to practice for our Friday night church bowling league. Joyce was one of the best women bowlers, boasting a season average of 161. When I asked my question, though, she took a puzzled look at her feet. Inwardly she was saying, *Which foot do I lead with?* Then she tried to bowl.

As always she led with her left foot, but because she was thinking about her habit, it didn't feel right. This continued throughout most of the first game, a game in which Joyce rolled only 127. More and more she looked at her feet. Nothing felt right. Finally, by the end of the first game she had just about managed to return to normal.

When she again felt confidence in her bowling, she fixed her gaze on me and declared, "Chuck, never do that to me again!" We all laughed as she spoke. She joined us. We all saw the trouble you can get into when you think too much about how you do things that are habits.

What Is a Habit?

A habit is a behavior that:
1. is well-established;
2. is part of a *pattern* of behavior;
3. requires little or no thought;
4. is acquired through repetition.

15

Let's look at the various components of this definition, because each one is important at different points in this book.

First, a habit is well-established.

In a sense, this is simply saying that a habit is a habit. But I want to do more. A habit is *your customary way of responding to a situation,* whether tying your shoes, greeting a long-absent friend, or disciplining a child.

This means that a habit is far more than most people think. We generally think of habits more narrowly, as isolated patterns of behavior that stand out for attention. We need to think about habits, however, as our customary ways of responding to any situations we face repeatedly.

A habit is also a pattern of behavior rather than an isolated act.

Most people think of a habit as event "H." I want you to think of a habit as a pattern of response. This means event "H" is preceded by events D-E-F-G and followed by events I-J-K-L. For example, each time Samson got into trouble in the Old Testament, it was because he was involved with a non-Israelite woman. But as we look more closely, we see that before he actually got involved with the Philistine women, he had first wandered around the countryside of Philistia admiring them. Also, once he got involved, he always seemed to provoke conflicts, conflicts he appeared to have liked, because they helped him embarrass the Philistines. In a modern example, I arrive late for church each week because I stay up later than normal on Saturday night, I get out of bed later than usual on Sunday morning, and I know I can be late to church without being penalized as I would be at work or school. Unless your perspective on habits is broader than people have customarily thought, you'll have a difficult time breaking your bad habits. You need the Holy Spirit's help in discovering these patterns.

Habits are also patterns of behavior requiring little or no thought.

Of course, this is one of the great values of habits. They make life easier for you by eliminating the need to think in situations you face frequently. We can readily see the problems people have when they lose basic habits through senility or a stroke. Suddenly they forget how to do simple tasks they used to do automatically.

Finally, habits are patterns of behavior acquired through repetition.

God created habits as a means of easing our effort in dealing with repetitive situations. However, repetition by itself is not enough. You can repeat some nonsense behavior as often as you want, and you won't create a habit.

Habits result from the combination of some need with a behavior you repeat each time you want to satisfy that need. The stronger the need, the stronger your habit will become through repetition. In addition, the stronger the need, the more difficult it will be to break the habit if you decide you want to change. Generally speaking, habits also increase in strength as they are repeated. As a result, the longer you have a habit, the harder it is to break it. Finally, all these principles apply just as much to bad habits as they do to good ones. Although God instituted the habit principle into your life, it is up to you to use it for your benefit.

Why do we keep bad habits even when we know they are bad? They continue for two basic reasons. First, they meet needs in our lives. This is probably the most basic reason why they endure. If they met no need, we would drop them.

Second, habits endure because we naturally resist change. It took God almost sixty years to get Jacob to stop his scheming, even though he must have seen on occasion how much trouble it caused him. Even if we learn about a better way of satisfying our needs, we will probably stick with our old habits because they are comfortable. Paul expressed his frustration with this when he said in Romans 7:21, "It seems to be a fact of life that when I want to do what is right, I inevitably do what is wrong." It is simply easier to keep doing something that is only partially effective than it is to change to something better. We prefer a known demon to the unknown. We naturally resist change, and thus our habits endure.

Habits fall into four categories. The most obvious are *physical habits*, such as tying your shoes the same way each time, eating with the same utensils, or always driving the car the same way. All these habits involve basically physical skills that make life easier.

More complex are *social habits*. You respond in habitual ways to the announcement of an engagement, news of a friend's

---

Types of Habits

1. **Physical habits** (shoe tying, eating, teeth brushing).
2. **Social habits** (introductions, birth announcements, responses to death).
3. **Emotional habits** (joy, anger, sorrow, excitement).
4. **Chemical habits** (drugs, alcohol, caffeine, nicotine, sugar).

---

death, the introduction of a stranger, or the presence of someone either socially superior or inferior. Even Paul began most of his letters with the same basic format: "Paul to church/person, greetings." Your responses are more complex than physical habits, but again they are habits that make life easier, because they eliminate the need to think about what you will do, and they smooth relations between people.

Even more complex are *emotional habits*, such as responding in anger when someone prevents you from doing what you want, when someone treats you unfairly, or when you see a child mistreated. You also respond with love in some situations, with enthusiasm in others, and with joy in still others. Your emotional responses are complex, drawn out in response to who you are in situations too complex to define, but they are just as much habit as your physical habits. They are well-established, require no thought, and have been acquired through repetition.

Finally, we face *chemical habits*. In this book I don't want to deal in great detail with chemical habits, even though I will mention them occasionally. The basic principles outlined here will work, but chemical habits are very complex because they involve substance dependency (or addiction, as we commonly call it) in combination with both emotional and social habits. The physical dependency on the chemical is difficult enough to overcome by itself, but deep-seated emotional needs, such as feelings of inferiority or insecurity, and deep-seated social needs, such as the need to belong and be well thought of by friends, are also involved. Anyone with a strong chemical habit probably needs professional assistance to break free, even though many people can overcome lesser chemical dependencies, such as addiction to caffeine or nicotine, without professional help.

Habits and Christian Living

How does all this relate to Christian living? The first thing you need to recognize is that habits themselves are neither good nor bad. I have already said that God established the habit principle in our lives. You now have to decide how to use it. You can use it for good by making a habit of daily devotions, or for ill by engaging in habits that displease God and cause problems for yourself.

You also need to realize that a bad habit is not necessarily a sin. Many bad habits limit your effectiveness in dealing with other people, but it is wrong to call them a sin. Others are a social embarrassment, but they aren't a sin. What if you bite your fingernails, chew your cheek, don't bathe enough, sound like a horse while eating, keep a sloppy house, or tell corny jokes? Are those sins? I don't think so. But it is a good idea to change, because those habits bother other people and hinder your Christian witness and ministry. You need to be careful to make this distinction. Sinful habits deserve prompt attention. Other bad habits can be put off until later. You need to focus on what is most important for your Christian development and ministry.

We want to be very practical in our treatment of habits. For the purpose of this book, a bad habit is any habit that causes more problems than it solves. Even more specifically, a bad habit is any habit you decide you want to break, whatever, your reasons might be.

3

Self-Talk

My son Peter walked into the bedroom where Geri, my wife, was working. He stood staring at his mother for a moment, then questioned, "Mommy, are you talking to *yourself*?" He was puzzled by the fact that she was talking even though she was in the room alone.

What Peter heard was simply the outward expression of what each of us does continually. We all carry on continuous conversations with ourselves. The average public speaker speaks at 100 to 200 words per minute. Casual conversation is carried on at about 100 words per minute. But psychologists have discovered that each of us carries on an internal conversation that goes at about 1200 to 1500 words per minute. Because we often talk with ourselves in pictures rather than actual words, we may be carrying on our internal conversations at thousands of words per minute. What significance does this have?

This conversation determines how you behave.

The words you say inside your head, the pictures you paint for yourself that no one else ever sees, determine how you behave. If someone approaches you and says, "I want you to give the devotions next week when our club meets," your mind immediately begins to work at high speed. It may be saying, *Oh, no I can't do that. I've failed every time I've done that in the past.* Or it may create a picture of one particular time when you stood up in front of a group, poorly prepared, highly nervous, and made such a fool of yourself that you simply can't forget it.

That picture immediately gives you the courage to say,

"No, I'm sorry, but I can't speak in public." You refuse even to try because of your internal conversation. That conversation is called *self-talk*. Its existence explains a lot of behavior that otherwise seems inexplicable.

Using this concept, let's examine Peter's denial of Jesus. What we see in the gospels are three different occasions when Peter denied he knew Jesus. Outwardly these situations were inexplicable based on Peter's past behavior. He was a loyal disciple. What could ever cause him to deny his master? But inside, Peter was probably saying something like, *I want to be near Jesus, but if they discover I'm a disciple, they'll probably arrest me as well as Him. I'm only safe if no one discovers I'm a disciple. I'll do everything I can to keep in the shadows and watch from a distance. I'll have to be very careful.*

The gospel writers, however, confined themselves to describing outward behavior. So I am using my imagination to reconstruct what Peter might have said to himself and how such thinking could have led to his denials. It was not so much the questioning that caused problems for Peter as it was what he was thinking when he heard the questions. His self-talk explains his actions (though it doesn't excuse them).

Over the past twenty years, psychologists have closely examined human behavior to find out why we act as we do. They have found one key to our behavior in what we say to ourselves, our self-talk. Most people think they encounter something in their environment that we can call an activating event (A), and they then respond with their consequent behavior (C). But that's not true. The activating event (A) is first interpreted by their belief systems (B), where they think about what is happening, and then they respond with the consequent behavior (C). It's as simple as A-B-C.

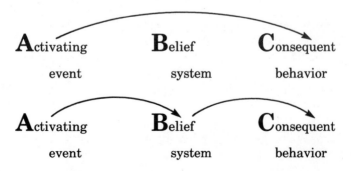

Activating   **B**elief   **C**onsequent

event   system   behavior

Activating   **B**elief   **C**onsequent

event   system   behavior

Principles of Self-Talk

1. Your thoughts create your emotions.
2. Your thoughts affect your behavior.
3. Your perceived center of control affects your behavior.
4. You generally think irrationally:
   overgeneralizing;
   labeling;
   emphasizing the negative over the positive;
   jumping to conclusions;
   thinking in absolutes.
5. You create change in your life by gaining control of your thoughts.

Five basic principles support and explain self-talk and the subsequent behavior.

First, *your thoughts create your emotions.*

Most people think this is the other way around. In fact, psychologists don't even agree fully. Some of them believe that when we are sad we think sad thoughts and when we are happy we think happy thoughts. But it's not that simple. Let me illustrate. Sit back for a moment. Close your eyes. Now take a minute and make yourself sad as you sit there quietly. After you've done that, next make yourself happy as you continue to relax there in your chair.

Let's analyze what you just did. How did you make yourself happy or sad? Most people immediately respond, "I thought about _____, which made me happy/sad." That's right. But let's look more closely at your situation. Did anything around you change while you were thinking about the event that made you happy or sad? No? Then what caused the change? That's right. Your thoughts. Thus, you proved for yourself that it is your thoughts that create your emotions, and not the other way around. Because angry feelings, anxiety, and feelings of social pressure play a key role in habit-generating moods, it's important for you to lock this principle securely in your mind.

Second, *your thoughts affect your behavior.*

Even though you might not always realize it, or even want

to admit it, your thoughts determine how you behave. Let's imagine you come home after a trying day. As you get out of the car, you say to yourself, *Am I beat. All I want to do is take it easy this evening.* When you walk through the door, the kids greet you with "Can we go swimming? Bobby invited us over to his house to go swimming tonight. Please, can we go swimming?" Inside, you are telling yourself how tired you are and how much you want to relax this evening. Taking the kids swimming at Bobby's is not your idea of a relaxing evening. You say no.

You hardly settle into your favorite chair for the evening when Frank calls. He, Paul, and Tom plan to play nine holes of golf after dinner. Why don't you take a shower to refresh yourself and come join them on the golf course? Suddenly your tiredness is gone. *This is relaxing!* you think. If you really look closely at what is going on, you will discover that the difference is in what you are telling yourself. You're tired when the kids want to go swimming, because that is not your idea of relaxation. Although physically nothing has changed, you're refreshed by the thought of a round of golf. Your thoughts greatly affect your behavior, determining what you will do.

Third, *your perceived center of control affects your behavior.*

Inside you, we might say, are many different control centers. As you encounter various situations, different control centers come into play. When asked to do something you know how to do and enjoy doing, your confidence center comes into play. When asked to join the church visitation committee and go calling on new people in the community, your shyness center comes into play. Whatever center you *think* applies to the situation you are facing will be the one to take charge. Each center has specified thoughts it applies to your situation. It may apply your shyness thoughts, your tiredness thoughts, or your lack-of-confidence thoughts. On the other hand, it may apply your known-social-skills thoughts, your feeling-of-being-refreshed thoughts, or your confidence thoughts. You then respond to the situation with the thoughts you have previously learned, because you perceive the need for this control center to be activated. And your thoughts in turn control your behavior based on your judgement of which center should take control.

Let me illustrate from my relationship with dogs. As a

child I was bitten by a large dog, and since then, any time I face a large dog, I become quite frightened. However, I once owned a large dog for about two years, and dealing with him never frightened me. In fact, I romped and played hard with him without a trace of fear. The reason I could do this lay in my control center. When I encountered Prince, my I'm-going-to-have-fun control center came into play. But, when I encounter a strange, large dog, my look-out-he-might-hurt-you center comes into play. My thoughts at the sight of a dog determine how I will respond.

Having shown how your thoughts affect your behavior, we come now to the stinger, the fourth self-talk principle: *you generally think irrationally*, particularly when dealing with bad habits.

I can imagine someone saying, "Now hold on there. That may be true for most people, but it's certainly not true for me." But let's reserve judgement until all the evidence is in.

In our American society, particularly in the evangelical church, we pride ourselves on the fact that we think rationally. Yet the Bible itself says, "The heart is the most deceitful thing there is, and desperately wicked. No one can really know how bad it is! Only the Lord knows! He searches all hearts and examines deepest motives so He can give to each person his right reward, according to his deeds — how he has lived" (Jer. 17:9-10). David, the man after God's own heart, prayed, "Search me, O God, and know my heart; test my thoughts. Point out anything You find in me that makes You sad, and lead me along the path of everlasting life" (Ps. 139:23-24). These verses suggest that our thoughts may not be nearly so rational as we like to imagine. Let's look at some common examples of irrational thinking.

Probably the most common form of irrational thinking is *overgeneralization*.

We jump all over children when they say "Everybody does it," but we do the same thing. In overgeneralizing, you take a single instance and turn it into a universal truth. Job's friends did this with his disasters. They looked at what was happening to him and generalized, "God is punishing you for your sin." It is true that God punishes people for their sin, but they over-generalized and concluded that any time anyone is experiencing hardship, that is punishment for sin.

I experienced this when in 1978 I left a pastoral position under unpleasant circumstances. In the days immediately following my departure, I kept telling myself, *You're a failure*. But I soon realized that was not the case. I was a failure at one job with one church. But I could point to many other areas of success in my life. I slowly learned to tell myself when I got to thinking "down" thoughts, *You may have failed as a minister of education at this church, but that does not make you a failure*. Frequently, however, we generalize in this manner, jumping from a single instance to a universal declaration.

A special form of generalization we all fall into is *labeling*.

We label people, events and situations in such a way that we expect certain things to be true or to happen, and other things not to happen. In John 4, Jesus and His disciples traveled through Samaria. When they stopped at Jacob's well, Jesus sent the disciples into town for food. While He waited for them to return, a woman approached the well to draw water. Jesus engaged her in conversation, and she eventually responded in faith. However, as Jesus was talking with her, the disciples returned from their grocery shopping. They were astonished that Jesus was talking with this woman. Why? They prejudicially labeled a woman as someone who is not able to understand spiritual matters, and they labeled all Samaritans as those who refuse to believe in God.

It must be said that some labeling is necessary. Think of the confusion that would result if labels could not be used. But labels can also distort our perception of circumstances. I once interviewed for a rural church position, and I was rejected. About a year later I happened to meet the same church official who had turned me down, and we sat and talked for about half an hour. As we finished our conversation, he told me, "I made a mistake in dealing with you last year. I thought a man as interested in writing and studying as you are simply couldn't work with rural people. I now know I was wrong."

He labeled me "intellectual" because of my interests and drew a certain conclusion from that: "He can't work with rural people." Later, he learned that his label didn't really fit and had caused him to make a mistaken judgement. In the same way, if you label yourself with "controlled by a bad habit," you can create a situation you can't break out of because of the label.

Another form of irrational thinking is the tendency to *emphasize the negative over the positive.*

Even the prophet Elijah did this following his great victory on Mount Carmel over the prophets of Baal. When Queen Jezebel reprimanded him and threatened to execute him for what he did, he immediately turned and fled into the desert. There he complained to God that, in all Israel, he alone was faithful to Him. He focused on the problem caused by Jezebel and forgot about the great victory God had just given through his hands.

Today, listen to people talking about trying to lose weight. Do they relate their many successes during the past week? Rarely. What do they talk about? Their failures. They tell about one failure after another. In fact, they actually reward one another with special attention for telling a failure story. No one is rewarded for telling a success story. Thus, you can recognize your irrationality when you focus on the negative at the expense of the positive.

Jumping to conclusions is also a type of irrational thinking.

On one occasion, Jesus' disciples saw another group of men casting out demons. They quickly ran to tell Jesus and ask what they should do. Their immediate response was to get them to stop. They reasoned, "Since they aren't with us, they're against us." But Jesus challenged their conclusion.

I occasionally face similar reasoning in church. Once, when a couple returned from a long absence in the South, I specially welcomed their return to church. A few weeks later, I failed to observe the return of another member. After church a lady rebuked me, saying, "Ruthann was terribly hurt today when you slighted her."

In astonishment I replied, "Slighted her? How?"

"Why, you didn't recognize her from the pulpit as having been gone on vacation."

Immediately Ruthann had jumped to the conclusion that I didn't like her as much as the other people, because I had overlooked her return to church. We jump to conclusions like this in many areas of life without taking time to consider the alternatives.

Finally, irrational thinking often *takes an absolute form.*

We say, "I must . . ." or "I should . . ." or "I can't . . ." or "People should/shouldn't . . ." Most of the time when we feel hurt, slighted or injured, most of the time when we quit without trying, and much of the time when we feel guilty, we are making absolute statements using these words.

"I can't speak in public" is an absolute statement saying that under no circumstances can I speak in public. If your family's welfare suddenly depended on your ability to speak in public, however, you would learn. When you say "People shouldn't do that to me," you are saying, "I don't like people to do that to me" or "I want to control their behavior so I won't be hurt." But people don't always do what we like, and they are not under our control. Even God could not keep Adam and Eve from sinning once He gave them free will. Why should we assume others will always do what we want or that we can take control over their behavior?

In all your irrational thinking, you need to ask the Holy Spirit to help you learn how to challenge your thinking. Challenges form a significant portion of this book, so for now we will limit ourselves to four.

Challenges to Irrational Thinking

1. Is it really true?
2. Is my thinking biblical?
3. Can this be proved by independent observation?
4. Are there alternative ways of looking at this?

Challenge your irrational thinking with these four questions:

Is that really true? Many times, if you back off for a moment from your self-talk and analyze it, you will admit that it's not only not true, but it gives a false picture as well.

My wife and I have been struggling with this type of thinking for a while with one of our children. When we discipline him for something, he says, "You always treat me like a baby." If he could only see how we treat his brothers, he would realize we are just parents disciplining a child. What he says is not really true, but he tries to get away with things he shouldn't be doing by using that statement.

Is this thinking biblical? Often our thoughts simply contradict God's Word. By challenging yours, you bring them under God's control and get a more accurate picture of what you face.

It's not unusual for me to confront this type of thinking in premarital counseling. When I discover the couple has fallen into sexual patterns that violate God's Word, I challenge them. But they often respond, "We're in love and planning to be married, so what difference does it make?" Their thinking, however, is not biblical.

Can this be proved by independent observation? If you were someone else looking at this situation, would you come to the same conclusions you are now drawing? Many times, others view the situation in a different light.

I'm part of my denomination's task force on mediating church fights, particularly those in which the pastor is aligned against a portion of the congregation. Such fights often lead to statements that cannot be supported by independent observation. Harold stated in one confrontation, "The pastor's trying to spend the church into debt." When we asked for the supporting evidence for his statement, however, all he could produce were a few instances where the pastor made purchases Harold didn't like.

Are there alternative ways of looking at this? Remember the old fable of the blind men describing an elephant by touch? One who held the trunk argued that it was like a long, thick, rubber hose. Another, holding the tail, said it was more like a piece of rope. A third asserted it was more like a tree trunk — he was feeling a leg. The fourth told them they were all wrong because to him it felt like a large canvas tent when he touched its side. Try to see other people's points of view, the alternatives, before insisting on your own perspective.

The fifth principle of self-talk is that *you create change in your life by gaining control of your thoughts.*

If this book can be summarized in one statement, that is it. Learn to control your thoughts about your bad habit and you'll learn to control your bad habit. How do you do that? Put your negative thoughts on trial (using the methods already suggested and those that will follow).

Next, focus on what is good. Paul told us, "Fix your thoughts on what is true and good and right. Think about things that are pure and lovely, and dwell on the fine, good things in others. Think about all you can praise God for and be glad about" (Phil. 4:8).

There is an important reason for this. Since negative thoughts support your bad habits, you need to remove them. But simply removing them only leaves a vacuum. Thus, you need to squeeze them out with something better. The something better is your good thoughts. The more time you spend thinking about what is good, the less time you have to think about what is bad. In this way you slowly gain control of your thoughts and, therefore, of your behavior, your bad habit.

Finally, *learn the value of prayer and meditation.* Commit to memory the verses that have specific application to your habit. (For help in locating those verses, use *Nave's Topical Bible.*) The psalmist said, "How can a young man stay pure? By reading Your Word and following its rules ... I have thought much about Your Words, and stored them in my heart so that they would hold me back from sin" (Ps. 119:9,11). Joshua told the children of Israel, "Constantly remind the people about these laws, and you yourself must think about them every day and every night so that you will be sure to obey all of them. For only then will you succeed" (Josh. 1:8). Think often of these verses. Analyze them until you think you know everything possible about them. Then learn the specific verses on temptation as a means of defending yourself. Pray these verses as often as you need to, to build into your life the strength to resist temptation. God's Word is the Holy Spirit's tool in your life to fight temptation.

Become aware of your self-talk. As you engage in your bad habit, focus on what you are telling yourself in support of your habit. What are you saying when engaged in your habit? Afterward? The whole purpose of this chapter has been to make you sensitive to your self-talk so you can eventually gain control of it.

Assignment:

1. Listen to your self-talk for a few days. Write some of it down. Particularly note your self-talk when you are angry, frustrated, tense, or depressed. Then see how

it affects your behavior.

2. List the five basics principles of self-talk.

3. Write out the four challenges to irrational thinking. Keep them with you to challenge your self-talk.

Further reading:

David Stoop, *Self-Talk* (Chosen Books).

4

Changing Your Thought Life

"Gold. Gold. Mysterious powder that turns to gold," cried the patent medicine man. As a crowd gathered, he continued his cry until customers pushed forward. As he took each person's money, he whispered in his ear, "This powder will turn to gold when you mix it with water, but I must caution you. If you think about little red monkeys while you're mixing the powder and water, the magic won't work." Needless to say, everyone thought about little red monkeys as they mixed the powder with water. You just cannot *not* think about something.

This is why it's so important for a person who wants to break a habit to change his thinking. In the Bible, Paul calls this "renewing your mind." Romans 12:2 tells us that renewing our minds is part of the transformation of our lives. In the book of Proverbs we read, "As a man thinketh in his heart, so is he" (23:7 KJV).

In the last chapter we looked at the basic principles of self-talk. But our specific concern is self-talk as it applies to breaking a bad habit. So while you need to understand self-talk in general, I now want to make specific application to habit breaking.

Control

How do you apply this? To begin, you need to change your thinking about the behavior you want to change. Most of us see our bad habits as uncontrollable, but that is both labeling and focusing on the negative. Yet this is at least part of what most people mean when they say they have a bad habit — it

---

Needed Thought Changes

1. You have control of your habit most of the time (positive).
2. You fail occasionally, but you are not a failure (no labels).
3. Give yourself freedom to fail occasionally (no absolutes).
4. Focus on your successes (positive).
5. Challenge your excuses (challenges).
6. Recognize your rights.

---

is something they "can't control." It is something that holds them in bondage.

You need to change your thinking.

Instead of thinking of yourself as a person who has a bad habit, you need to think of yourself as a person who occasionally does something you don't want to do any more. Even if the "occasionally" is several times a day, you are saying you are not controlled by this behavior. Rather, you are a person who generally has self-control (a good label that focuses on your successes, on the positive), but who occasionally fails in that self-control.

Can you truthfully say this? Yes. Think for a moment of a compulsive habit such as gorging yourself until you vomit, a habit more common than most people realize. Careful examination shows that such a person has control five out of seven days each week. Further analysis shows that the control is even greater. The person has control all but three hours each week, failing only an hour and a half on those days when he or she does fail. Thus, of the 168 hours in the week, control is maintained for 165. Any habit can be subjected to this same analysis to show that periods of control are far greater than periods when control is lacking.

You spend more time each day in control than out of control. Occasionally, however, you fail. Paul tells us in Romans 6:14 that "sin need never again be your master, for now you are no longer tied to the law where sin enslaves you, but you are free under God's favor and mercy." This change in your thinking might seem minor, but it isn't. Your attitude toward yourself as a success or a failure is a key element in your ability to change.

Occasional Failures

Closely related to this is the folly of all-or-nothing thinking. Many people think of themselves as failures because they can't deal with their habits. Thus, when they slip once in their attempt to break a habit, they again declare themselves a failure (an overgeneralization and a negative label). Since further effort is futile if someone is a failure, they give up. That is wrong.

Tony is a classic example of this problem. For years he has been trying to quit smoking. Each time he starts with enthusiasm, planning all the things that will change when he is free of the habit. Things often go well for the first few days. On occasion he has even lasted a week or more. Then something comes up and Tony feels pressured. About that time a friend offers him a cigarette — so he can relax. As he smokes the cigarette, Tony tells himself, *You're horrible. You never do anything right. You're one of those people condemned to smoke for the rest of their lives. You're a failure.* He then goes out and buys a pack of cigarettes and smokes them all out of frustration and anger (but he is also proving his self-talk, *I'm a failure*). He is back into his habit because he is convinced that one slip makes him a chain-smoking failure.

Change, however, takes time. No one lives completely free of failures. Change also includes occasional failures *on the road to success*. This is true of any new behavior, no matter how simple.

Last weekend I took a friend cross-country skiing. Mike is an accomplished athlete, but he had never been skiing before. After he fell down a few times, I noted he was getting discouraged. He was facing a sport that for the time being was beating him. I commented, "Mike, don't let it get you down when you fall. Part of learning how to ski is learning to get up after you fall and try again." So he did. And eventually he did very well.

The same principle holds true for any attempt to learn new behavior, which is what you are doing when you break a bad habit. You won't win if you think in all-or-nothing categories. There is plenty of ground on the road between bondage to a habit and freedom from it.

Freedom

If this is true, you also need to give yourself the freedom to fail while trying to change, secure in the knowledge that you are still loved by God. Because many of the habits we seek to break are sin, people often feel as if they should move from bondage to freedom in a day. Any failure renews their sin and, they therefore conclude, alienates them from God.

But Romans 5:8-10 says:

> God showed his great love for us by sending Christ to die for us while we were still sinners. And since by His blood He did all this for us as sinners, how much more will He do for us now that He has declared us not guilty? Now He will save us from all God's wrath to come. And since, when we were His enemies, we were brought back to God by the death of His Son, what blessings He must have for us now that we are His friends, and He is living within us!

Paul wrote that to show how great God's love was for us during the time we were in rebellion against Him. Now we are His family! Surely He stands ready to forgive even when we fail.

This is why it's so important to understand the process Bill Bright calls spiritual breathing. First John 1:9 states, "If we confess our sins to Him, He can be depended on to forgive us and to cleanse us from every wrong. [And it is perfectly proper for God to do this for us because Christ died to wash away our sins]." When you sin, God wants you to exhale the impurities by confessing your failure and asking for His forgiveness. You then ask Him to cleanse you, purifying and renewing you for continued service. Then you ask Him to fill you with His Holy Spirit, and at that point you inhale, appropriating by faith that fullness of the Spirit of God. The broken relationship is restored. You need never live again with failure for more than the moment it takes to ask for forgiveness and a refilling with the Holy Spirit.

Because you are part of God's family, He has promised that

He will never again reject you for sinful behavior. Rather, He has committed Himself to creating in you the character of His Son, Jesus Christ. He knows you will occasionally fail. He knows you will fail often before you succeed in breaking many of your habits. Nevertheless, He always walks beside you to pick you up and help you start over again. Only by giving you the freedom to fail can He also give you the freedom to try to change. Since God gives you the freedom to fail without rejecting you, can't you give yourself the same freedom? Thus, you are freed from all-or-nothing thinking.

Success

When you're trying to break a bad habit, you tend to focus on your failures (concentrating on the negative). To counter this, you need to do some daydreaming. Imagine yourself in a successful battle with temptation. How do you do it? What does it feel like? Enjoy the sweet taste of victory for a moment — even if it is only in your imagination. Picture yourself in the worst possible temptation you face, and then imagine yourself victorious. As you visualize victory, it is easier to achieve victory. People who are winners invariably visualize themselves as victors.

In 1983, *Psychology Today* reported an interesting experiment with the power of one's thought life. The experimenters assembled a group of college students and divided them into three separate test groups. The first group practiced basketball free throws for an hour, then went home and promised not to touch a basketball for the next week. The second group practiced for an hour and then was instructed to go home and think about making free throws for one hour each day for a week. The final group practiced for one hour each day for a week. The following week, each group was tested again. It came as no surprise that those in the first group did no better than their previous efforts. The third group improved most, as would also be expected. Surprisingly, however, the people in the second group improved almost as much as those in the third by simply thinking about doing well. The psychologists conducting the experiment concluded that thinking about doing something well is almost as valuable as actually doing it.

In addition to dreaming of victory, dream about the benefits of giving up your habit. What would it be like to never again reach for an extra piece of cake, take another beer, accept more jobs than you can handle, or drive like a wild man through traffic? What benefits would come from giving up your habit? These are your goals. Keep them in front of you as you fight this battle. "Without a vision the people perish," said the author of Proverbs (29:18, KJV), and we also perish unless we can visualize the benefits of breaking our bad habits.

Excuses

A few days ago I was at the grocery store, waiting in the quick service line to check out. Suddenly a woman rushed up, moved in front of the line, and commented to whoever would listen, "I've got an appointment at the beauty parlor and I'm late." She then slapped a twenty-dollar bill on the counter with her items.

We let her go.

What happened in that situation? The woman knew she was doing something unacceptable. Her response was something many of us do when we know we're in the wrong. You get caught like that, and you make an excuse to whoever will listen. The excuse is a rationalization. You know you are doing something wrong. Everyone else knows you're doing something wrong. But you do it anyhow. You don't do it, however, without a few guilt feelings, so you give a rationalization to those who will listen. No one believes your rationalization is justification for what you're doing, but you give it anyhow, and everyone accepts your violation of acceptable behavior. You do the same thing in your self-talk with your bad habits. (This is a classic example of irrational thinking that won't stand up to the suggested challenges).

Every bad habit is supported by rationalizations. (Rationalizations are reasons — which you don't believe — that enable you to do what you know is wrong). Like everyone else, you have used them for years to justify (excuse) your behavior. You may even have used them so long that you now actually believe them yourself. However, when you take the time to examine them in the light of day with the suggested challenges, they are worthless. Yet so long as you have not developed counter-thoughts to overcome them, you will continue to be ruled by them. These rationalizations are part of your self-talk. Like the lady who wants to cut into the front of the line when she knows she shouldn't, you talk to yourself to excuse what you know you shouldn't do.

As you prepare to overcome your habit, you need to develop counter-thoughts (based on the challenges) for each of your rationalizations. Most of the time this is not difficult. You know that what you are telling yourself is false. It simply won't stand up to the challenge. You choose, however, to believe it because it is more convenient to continue believing it than to change your behavior. Now you want to change. This means you need to take each rationalization and challenge it as a means of developing counter-thoughts that you will use in the future to beat it down.

Jacob, whose very name meant "schemer," can help us see how rationalizations work. He tricked his brother, his father, and finally his uncle before God caught him in the pain of dealing dishonestly with people. We can imagine that he rationalized his scheming like this. *God promised before I was born that I was His special, chosen one. That must mean that the birthright is mine, even though Esau is older. Father shouldn't give the blessing to Esau since God said I would be more blessed than my brother, so I'm justified in tricking him into giving it to me instead. Uncle Laban cheated me by giving me Leah instead of Rachel and making me work without wages, so there's no reason why I shouldn't trick him out of some of his sheep. Besides, he has so many that he won't miss a few.* Challenge questions applied to his rationalizations would make each one useless. This is what you need to do with your own rationalizations.

Rationalizations can also hurt marriages. When Helen and Kevin came into my office for counseling, she said she had a deep-seated anger over the way he always put things off until the last minute. Sometimes this totally ruined their plans. But even when it didn't, Helen complained, it made it difficult for her to do her work.

As we explored Kevin's procrastination, various things came out. First, as soon as Helen began to push, he began to tell himself, *I'm not a man if I let her boss me around*, even though he admitted he did need occasional reminders. He also admitted that he always found an excuse to avoid doing what needed to be done. He said he generally told himself, *I'll have time tomorrow, so I don't need to do it today.* But experience never seemed to teach him that tomorrow might have interruptions that would make completing the task impossible.

He also said that he usually told himself, *That job's not too hard. You'll be able to finish it in no time once you get working on it.* But problems always seemed to come up that he hadn't anticipated, and the project took longer than planned. When Kevin confronted these rationalizations and realized their bad effects, he worked at developing counter-thoughts as a means of gaining control of his procrastination.

Write out the rationalizations you use. Beside each one write at least one counter-thought based on the challenge questions or your own thinking that proves it is wrong. Particularly use the challenge questions to help you.

Counter Thoughts (Examples)

My bad habit is driving too fast.

I support my habit with the following excuses:
1. I've only been ticketed twice in five years.
2. I need to make up time because I'm late.
3. Speedometers are set to register high.
4. I'm only keeping up with traffic.

My counter-thoughts are as follows:
1a. Even if I don't get caught, I'm still breaking the law.
1b. My driving is still a poor witness.
2a. I need to make sure to leave in plenty of time so I don't have to speed.
2b. It's better to be late than to break the law and hurt my witness.
3a. Where is the data to prove this?
3b. Since I don't know this for sure, I should observe the speed limit.
4a. Just because others are wrong doesn't mean I should be.
4b. Many drivers are observing the law.
4c. A Christian lifestyle should be distinctive.

Think Good

A few years ago I met JoAnn, a woman who impressed me as a wonderful person — but she was divorced. I later talked with her sister-in-law, Alice, about what happened. It seems that JoAnn's husband, Roy, was a man who always saw the dark side of life. On a sunny day he saw the single cloud in the sky. He married JoAnn for her good qualities, but over the years he began to notice *and dwell on* her faults. Eventually he focused so strongly on her faults that he lost sight of her positive qualities. He then found a much younger woman and left with her.

You need to learn to counter negative thoughts with positive ones. When you are trying to break a habit, you tend to focus on the bad rather than the good. You dwell on the one failure in the week when you have had six days of success. You dwell on the one piece of cake you ate and fail to think about the many you haven't eaten. You dwell on your one swear word and forget about the days of clean language. Paul told us to fix our thoughts on things that are true and good and right. You need to counter each negative thought about your slips with positive thoughts about your successes. You can't change what has happened, but you can change the focus of your thinking about it.

Jeff showed me the value of this one weekend when I took a couple of friends skiing. We planned the trip all winter, but each time our plans were ruined by either too much new snow or bitter cold. Finally, things worked out so we could go. Our travel took a little more than an hour. When we arrived, we set out to cross-country ski about fourteen miles of hilly, wooded, northern Michigan terrain.

We had not gone a mile when Jeff broke the tip of his ski. We looked at it with disappointment. But at the same time we were thankful. The ski could have broken six miles out in the wilderness. Had that happened, Jeff would have had to walk back to the car in almost two feet of crusted snow. The trip would have been agony.

Jeff could have been upset with the ruined trip, but he was thankful instead for the early break that prevented a major problem. In the same way, you need to learn to look for alternative perspectives on your problems.

A biblical means of renewing your mind is learning how to see life from God's perspective. You do this by building as much of God's Word into your minds as you can. God told Isaiah, "For just as the heavens are higher than the earth, so are My ways higher than yours, and My thoughts than yours" (Isa. 55:9). This means you take the time to memorize key verses that apply to your problem. (Again, *Nave's Topical Bible* can help you locate them.)

In some instances, this means memorizing verses that have direct application to your habit. In others, you select verses that have general application. Sometimes you memorize verses that relate to the problems that cause tension in your life, verses dealing with anger, fear, or worry. Above all, you memorize verses that tell you of God's continuing love for you even when you fail. You want to know from His Word that He will continue loving you even though winning over your habit will take time. Memorization and meditation on applicable Bible verses is an important step in renewing your mind. In this way you learn to think God's thoughts about your habit, to gain His perspective. (For more on this, see Jim Downing's book *Meditation*, published by Navpress.)

Rights

When you are trying to break a habit, the issue of personal rights sometimes comes into play. By this I mean that many Christians seem to think they don't have the right to stand up to others except on matters that are strictly biblical. Thus, for example, you may be trying to stop overeating. But if a friend invites you to dinner at a restaurant where you know you will eat too much, you may feel uncomfortable about refusing. The thinking behind this notion is that Christians ought always to put the wishes of others before their own, that they should never be offensive or disagreeable unless the matter in question is obvious and flagrant sin.

If you are going to gain victory over your habit, however, you have to develop the attitude that as a Christian you *do* have rights. Some of the rights that affect habit breaking follow:

1. You have the right to judge what is best for you and to be responsible for the consequences.
2. You have the right to act without defending or justifying your actions to others. (For a full explanation of this, please see my book *Assertiveness and the Christian*.)
3. You have the right *not* to conform to others' expectations for you.
4. You have the right to change your mind.
5. You have the right to your feelings, opinions, and desires.
6. You have the right to be treated as fairly as others.

Unless you convince yourself that you have the right to act in your own best interests while trying to break your habit, you will find friends and relatives putting pressure on you that will keep you from your goals. Friends and relatives are often a major obstacle to change if you do not know and act on your assertive rights. Convince yourself that resisting social pressure is not wrong. In fact, at the present time it is just what you need to do.

Assignments:

1. Memorize Philippians 4:8-9.
2. Write out the rationalizations you use to support your habit.
3. Write out a challenge for each rationalization.
4. Learn your assertive rights, particularly those that apply to breaking your habit.

Further reading:

Charles Cerling, *Assertiveness and the Christian* (Tyndale).

5

Motivation to Change

Tom's father had been riding him for almost a year about his attitude. Since he turned sixteen he had been supercritical, complaining about everything. No matter what the family did, ate, or said, Tom had some negative comment to make. The family, particularly his parents, were fed up with him. His father, however, couldn't convince him that people don't like a person with a negative attitude. Then Tom began to change, and before long the constant complaining was gone.

After a week of the new Tom, his father tentatively asked, Why the sudden change?"

Tom related, "Do you remember our last church fellowship dinner? I sat next to old Mr. Hample. He spent the night telling me how bad things were. I tried to change the conversation several times, but every time I tried, he just had something negative to say. Suddenly it dawned on me — This is me a few years from now if I keep on being negative about everything. That did it. I decided right then to change."

Without motivation from within, Tom never would have changed. Family might have pressured him, but until he decided to change, nothing worked. Once he made a decision to change, change was possible.

Nothing is more important in change than motivation, a complex set of beliefs and attitudes related to your desire to change. All the tools and techniques plus the best counselors in the world will be useless unless you believe change is necessary and you are willing to make enough effort to change. On the other hand, if you have sufficient motivation, you probably won't need tools and counselors. You'll find some way to make it on your own.

Most of us don't have that much motivation. So we use a combination of motivation and help from others. This chapter is designed to help you develop sufficient motivation to change. While reading it, ask the Holy Spirit to give you that desire to change as you see your habit in a new light.

Benefits of Change

What benefits will you get if you change your bad habit? George had to ask this question. When he came in for counseling because his temper was threatening to destroy his family, he knew his wife had spoken with their lawyer. His kids hardly ever stayed home, because they were afraid he would explode. He was a big man, and as a teenager he learned that he could get almost anything by getting angry. If he really got angry, he picked up things and threw them, scaring the wits out of anyone nearby.

Now he was frightened. His anger gave him control over everyone around him. Many were too afraid to come near him. Those who did walked carefully lest he blow up. The problems growing out of his anger, however, were beginning to grow too large for him to handle. He struggled with what would happen if he gave up his anger. For the first time in years, he would not be able to control people except by persuading them. Since he was not a good talker, he was concerned that others might take advantage of him.

He also struggled with the question of how he would benefit from giving up his anger. He felt that he would probably develop a closer relationship with his wife. He also thought he might gain more friends, since he had discovered that people don't like to be near an angry man. He felt that if he did give it up, he might develop a closer relationship with his children, too, but he was concerned he might have waited too long. He knew he would feel less guilt, because he would not be stomping on people as often. He also felt he would gain a feeling of control in his life. At that point he felt out of control, governed by what happened around him rather than by what he really wanted. As he saw the list and the value of the items on it, his enthusiasm for breaking his habit grew. Below is a sample benefits list related to another habit, a common one.

Bad Habit: dominating most conversations

BENEFITS IF BROKEN:
1. I will learn more by listening.
2. My witness will improve, because people won't think I'm so proud.
3. Others won't avoid me.
4. I'll get to know others better by hearing about their experiences.
5. I'll be more relaxed by not having to think about what I'll say next.
6. I won't get dirty looks for interrupting others.

What benefits will you receive from giving up your habit? Take a moment and write them out. Seek God's wisdom to discover as many as possible and to see their value compared with current problems growing out of your habit.

Do You Want to Change?

Do you really want to change? This is the biggest hurdle I have to overcome with some counselees. They come to me with a problem, something disturbing them. They *tell* me they want to change, but when I suggest solutions, they only give half-hearted effort. They don't really want to change. Even though it gives them some discomfort, they enjoy their bad habit too much to give it up. They just want me to reduce the pain to a tolerable level. At this point, confirm your desire to really change as you read this chapter.

Benefits Gained by Your Habit

We've looked at the benefits of change. But what are the benefits you currently receive from your habit? We have habits for reasons. They meet needs. In some way you receive a reward, a payoff, when you engage in your habit. To overcome the habit, you need to see what those rewards are so that you can plan more effective ways of receiving the same benefits. To do that, let's look at what needs your habit meets.

Does your habit reduce tension for you? Common habits like fingernail biting, gum chewing, hair twisting, knuckle cracking, anger, walking away from problems and conflicts, and excessive eating do this. Each of them in its own way is a means of relieving tensions or nervousness.

Does your habit overcome fear? Many people use a critical spirit to overcome their own fears. Underlying their action is reasoning like this: *I'm not really sure of myself. People might not like me if they really knew me. If I criticize others, people won't look at me, because they're thinking about these others.* Thus, by criticizing others they hide their fear of being found out. They hide their own insecurity. Habits as different as anger, shyness, talkativeness, and perfectionism often hide fears.

Does your habit enable you to control others? Worry, depression, and anger often meet this criterion. When a person is a known worrier, prone to depression, or easily upset, people avoid doing things that will "make" him worry, become depressed, or get angry. In this way he controls others. The same can be said for many other habits. By referring to your problems, you can keep others from doing things you don't want them to do, as in "Don't do that, it just makes me nervous."

Harriet had been hospitalized for depression on numerous occasions over the years, a ploy she used to control her family. When things didn't go her way in the family, she would get more and more depressed until they would rush her to the hospital emergency room, afraid she might commit suicide. She would then be hospitalized for a few days, given antidepressant medication, and generally permitted to rest. While she was in the hospital, the family would deal with the problem that "caused" her to go there. Since she let them know her solution before she left, they invariably decided in her favor because they wanted to "protect" her. The discerning counselor who called her bluff by telling the family they needed help to protect themselves against her attacks of depression received a brutal dressing down because she didn't like being found out.

Does your habit make you the center of attention? Lateness, a critical spirit, a drinking problem, procrastination, bitterness, dominating conversations, always winning at one-upsmanship, knuckle cracking — all in their own ways draw attention to the person who has the habit. Many people feel they can't get a group's attention through other means, so they regularly come into a meeting late, crack their knuckles during a silent period, drink to the point where they have to be watched, or smoke so much that it draws others' attention to them. A critical or bitter spirit is always a way of making others notice them.

Does your habit free you from obligations to others? A few years ago, a couple came in for counseling for marriage problems. Every few months, Henry would have a "mental breakdown" in which he would empty the family bank account, disappear for a few days of unrestricted fun, be caught by the police and taken to the local hospital's mental health unit (which was like a nice motel), and then be released into the custody of his family a few weeks later. His "illness" meant that his wife took care of all financial matters in their marriage, since he couldn't be trusted with money.

The second time this occurred while I was counseling him, I went to the hospital to visit. As we talked, I said to Henry, "I think you have a pretty good thing going here. You hate your work, but if you just walked out on your job every few months you would be fired. Your income is too low to afford many fun times or a vacation. You don't like the responsibilities of a wife and family. So every few months you have a breakdown. You flee work that you hate anyhow. You use money you couldn't use under normal circumstances to have a good time you really can't afford. You then get a nice vacation in the hospital, where you are free to enjoy all the benefits of hospital life. You do all this without any penalties, because you had a breakdown. I wish I could cop out that easily."

While I said this, Henry sat there like a little child caught with his hand in the cookie jar. When I finished, he looked at me and said, "You're the first counselor who's seen through me. I guess I'm going to have to develop a new routine."

Many habits are used, often unintentionally, to free us from obligations to others. A tension headache, anger, inability to handle stress, worry, depression, drinking, and many other things can become habits used to avoid responsibility.

List the benefits you gain from your habit. David prayed in Psalm 139:23, 24, "Search me, O God, and know my heart; test my thoughts. Point out anything You find in me that makes You sad, and lead me along the path of everlasting life." Ask the Holy Spirit to show you why you behave as you do, since sin is often quite subtle. Below is a sample list of benefits a person might get from a bad habit.

Bad Habit: overspending my income

BENEFITS:
1. It feels good to spend money.
2. People like the things I buy or do for them.
3. I feel important buying things for others.
4. The things I buy make me feel important.
5. The things I buy impress others.
6. I hate to budget.

Problems Caused by Your Habit

Now I want you to list the problems created by your habit. For example, what are the negative effects of worrying. Worry causes stomach problems, it contributes to high blood pressure, and it causes digestive and elimination problems. It also makes it difficult to concentrate on what you are doing. It keeps your life in turmoil. It hinders your relationship with God and your ability to minister for Him.

Now, list the problems your particular habit causes, just as we have done with worry.

But your habit doesn't just cause problems for you. It also causes problems for other people. List the problems it causes others. Again, let's use worry as our example. If I worry, I'm often unable to meet the obligations I have toward others. Worry upsets others around me. My worry can depress others as I talk with them. Worry makes it difficult for my spouse to get along with me. Worry makes it difficult for me to be an effective parent. Worry cuts down on my efficiency at work. Other results could be listed. Now list the effects of your own habit on others. If you can see the extent of the trouble your habit causes, you will be better motivated to give it up.

God's Word

What does the Bible say about your habit? Well, it could be that it says nothing directly. Many of our habits aren't mentioned in the Bible. If you bite your fingernails, you won't find a reference to that in the Bible. The same goes for twisting your hair, cracking your knuckles, procrastination, even smoking, and many others. A number of bad habits, however, *are* addressed directly in the Bible. If you are critical of others, the Bible talks about that. If you get angry too easily, the Bible tells you that is wrong. If you are prone to worry, the Bible has much to say to you.

To find out what the Bible has to say about your particular habit, get a concordance and look up every reference in it. You might find it necessary to use a topical concordance such as the previously mentioned *Nave's Topical Bible.* This type of concordance doesn't simply list words in the Bible; it also lists subjects. It might help when a regular word concordance wouldn't.

Don't overlook books written on the topic of specific habits. Most major bad habits are the subject of complete books. Anger, worry, frustration, overeating — all these and more have been addressed by recognized authorities. It would be foolish not to make use of them to get God's perspective on your problem.

Others with Your Habit

The next step is for you to describe how others who have your habit look or sound. Often you can't really see or hear yourself, but you can observe others who share your habit. Let's use lateness as an example. The person who is tardy often looks chagrined when he enters a meeting. He is embarrassed because of what he has done to others. He feels guilty because he made them wait for him. He feels defensive about what has happened; therefore, he has a hard time being at ease with other people. He disrupts the meeting when he arrives late.

When others engage in your habit, how do they look and sound to you?

Finally, what problems will changing create? When George thought about giving up anger as a means of controlling others, he saw that it would greatly reduce his power over them. It would force him to think more. It would make him interact more with people rather than bullying them.

Change is going to create problems as well as solve them. What problems will change create for you? Write them out.

While going through these processes, seek God's wisdom. In James 1:5 we read, "If you want to know what God wants you to do, ask Him, and He will gladly tell you, for He is always ready to give a bountiful supply of wisdom to all who ask Him; He will not resent it." We often keep bad habits because we really don't see the problems they create or the benefits of change. Ask the Holy Spirit to help you see what you really are doing, and what you can gain by giving it up, as a means of motivating you to change.

Contributing Problems

Before we conclude, we need to look at one more question. Are more serious problems contributing to your bad habit? Maybe the habit you want to give up is not the source of your problem but simply an indication of a greater problem. You would be surprised at the number of problems that grow out of a poor self-image. Overeating, anger, worry, depression and shyness are all results of a low estimate of one's worth. If this is your situation, you should deal with the more serious problems first. (If you have a poor self-image, you should read Josh McDowell, *His Image...My Image*. Other helpful authors are Maurice Wagner, Bruce Narramore, and Norman Wright. Each has key insights into overcoming a poor self-image.)

Problems that won't go away easily are often surface problems with deeper roots. So if you struggle for a long time with a habit and still can't defeat it, you may have deeper problems you need to deal with. If you use the techniques provided in this book for a long time and get no results, you probably need more help than this book can give you. (For minor habits, a month is a long time. For major habits, think in terms of a year.)

You want to change, but you've tried and had problems in the past. Even now you may question your ability to succeed. Fine. It's wise to recognize potential problems and face them. But we've also looked in detail at your motivation to change. We've seen that motivation means more than almost anything else. This chapter gives various sources for motivation. As you examine these sources, you should be sufficiently motivated to try again — but this time, with proper motivation, you can succeed.

Assignments:

1. List the benefits of change.
2. List the benefits you gain from your habit.
3. List the problems your habit causes.
4. Write out what the Bible says about your habit (if anything).
5. Describe one other person with your habit (if you can).
6. Memorize James 1:5.

Further Reading:

D. G. Kehl, *Control Yourself* (Zondervan)

6

God's Teaching about Temptation

Following the birth of their children, most women struggle with a weight problem. My wife, Geri, has struggled along with others, but she has discovered a solution for herself. She refuses to keep sweets around the house. Instead she keeps a good supply of popcorn (which she rarely eats with butter) and fresh fruit. When asked about the lack of sweets in the house, she comments, "If they're around I'll eat them, so I don't keep them around."

To beat a bad habit, you need to know the forms temptation takes. There are two steps in this process: learning what God says about temptation; and the particular, unique nature of the temptations you face.

In his seminars, Bill Gothard tells us there are three battlegrounds for temptation: the arena of your thoughts, the arena of your actions, and finally, the arena of your habits. While you want to battle temptation at the level of your habits, we also want to see what God has to say about temptation at all levels.

God Gives Strength

But remember this — the wrong desires that come into your life aren't anything new and different. Many others have faced exactly the same problems before you. And no temptation is irresistible. You can trust God to keep the temptation from becoming so strong that you can't stand up against it, for He has promised this and will do what He says. He will show you how to escape temptation's power so that you can bear up patiently against it (1 Cor. 10:13).

This may be the single most important verse in the Bible dealing with temptation. It says that no temptation you experience is new or unique. Many people have been tempted in the same way in the past.

This information is important, because like most people, you probably often feel that no one else has ever been where you are. You feel alone, isolated. If no one has been there before, then no one can help you. No one understands. Paul told us, however, that the people of the Old Testament give us examples of the trials of life: "All these things happened to them as examples — as object lessons to us — to warn us against doing the same things; they were written down so that we could read about them and learn from them in these last days as the world nears its end" (1 Cor. 10:11).

As I said earlier, throughout my teen years, I was plagued with what I believed were dirty thoughts. Some were dirty, but some were simply the normal reactions of a developing young man toward developing young women. Nonetheless, I felt devastated because I imagined that no one else could have thoughts as evil and wicked as my own.

During my late teens and early twenties, I slowly came to realize that all young men have problems with these thoughts. As I learned this, I felt free to discuss my struggles with other men. They told me of various means they used in dealing with these thoughts. My big original problem, however, was not my thoughts, but the feeling of isolation that came from them.

There is also a wonderful promise in this verse. God will not permit you to face a temptation that is more than you can stand. He protects you. He wants you to succeed. On the night before Peter denied Him, Jesus told Peter, "Simon, Simon, Satan has asked to have you, to sift you like wheat, but I have pleaded in prayer for you that your faith should not completely fail. So when you have repented and turned to Me again, strengthen and build up the faith of your brothers" (Luke 22:31,32). As Jesus declared Himself on Peter's side as he faced temptation, so He declares himself on your side as you face your temptations.

The attitude of my wife and myself toward our children's success illustrates this. Over the past couple of years, we have been attempting to teach our youngest son, Peter, how to cross-country ski. Shortly after we bought him skis, we got into a situation that was way beyond his abilities. After that experience, we had to back up and take him to places that were really too easy for him in order to restore his lost confidence. We spent many hours working with him in that regard so he could again ski with pleasure instead of fear. Our goal has been to do everything we can to guarantee his success in what can be a difficult and frightening sport.

So it is with God. He protects you from temptations that would be more than you could take.

Finally, Paul told us that God creates an escape route from every temptation. Temptation never so traps us that we cannot avoid sinning. There's always a way out. It may be necessary to literally run from temptation, as Joseph did when tempted by Potipher's wife (Gen. 39:7-18), but there will always be a way of escape. Some of those ways of escape will be described later in this book.

A recently married man found a way out of gambling. Mitch is such a highly competitive young man that he just can't seem to pass up the simplest challenge. This wouldn't be so bad if he didn't consider each wager, no matter how insignificant, as one he has to take. As a single man with little money, such an attitude meant no serious problems. But when Mitch got married, his habit created major problems. Things the family needed went unpurchased because he had used the money gambling. Yet he felt trapped into it. Whenever someone even casually mentioned a bet, Mitch jumped in and took on the wager. He felt he had no means of escape.

Then Mitch discovered the promise of 1 Corinthians 10:13. It still wasn't easy to resist temptation, but he felt that God led him to meet gambling offers with the simple statement, "Now that I'm married, I have to use my money for family. I'm sorry, but I can't take you up on that any more." He took some not-too-pleasant kidding at first about being henpecked, but once people realized he was serious, they simply quit challenging him. He didn't know it, but it had become a game with his friends to see who could catch him with the silliest bet.

Jesus Understands our Temptations

Then Jesus was led out into the wilderness by the Holy Spirit, to be tempted there by Satan. For forty days and forty nights He ate nothing and became very hungry.

Then Satan tempted Him to get food by changing stones into loaves of bread.

"It will prove You are the Son of God," he said.

But Jesus told him, "No! For the Scriptures tell us that bread won't feed men's souls: obedience to every word of God is what we need."

Then Satan took Him to Jerusalem to the roof of the temple. "Jump off," he said, "and prove You are the Son of God; for the Scriptures declare 'God will send His angels to keep You from harm,' . . . they will prevent You from smashing on the rocks below."

Jesus retorted, "It also says not to put the Lord your God to a foolish test!"

Next Satan took Him to the peak of a very high mountain and showed Him all the nations of the world and all their glory. "I'll give it all to You," he said, "if You will only kneel and worship me."

"Get out of here, Satan," Jesus told him. "The Scriptures say, 'Worship only the Lord God. Obey only Him.' "

Then Satan went away, and angels came and cared for Jesus. (Matt. 4:1-11)

This High Priest of ours [Jesus Christ] understands our weaknesses, since He had the same temptations we do, though He never once gave way to them and sinned. (Heb. 4:15).

Both these passages teach that Jesus Christ knows what it means to be tempted. Jesus knows the tremendous power of temptation. We might illustrate this with a question: Who exerts the greatest effort, the fighter who wins some and loses some, or the fighter who takes on the best the world has to offer and still comes out a winner? The answer is the one who always wins, of course. It doesn't take great effort to lose. So Jesus, who always won in His battles with temptation, has experienced the force of temptation far beyond what you and I ever will. He knows what it means to experience the full force of Satan's power, something we never have to face.

Jesus also knows the varieties of temptation you face. Jesus was tempted by Satan at this point in His life in three major areas of human experience that represented what He would face in the future. During His life He was tempted in all the common areas of human weakness, as Satan used every trick in his repertoire. As a result, there is never a temptation you face in which Jesus has not already felt temptation's power. He knows your every need and can meet them all.

Jesus also knows the subtlety of temptation. Satan commonly tempts people by distorting God's Word to his own ends. In every instance in Jesus' wilderness temptation, Satan twisted the Word of God to make Jesus think He could do Satan's bidding while also serving God. Such are many of your temptations. Thus, Jesus knows the subtlety of the temptations you face and can help you to victory over them.

These passages also show that Satan can be defeated. When you face temptation, you tend to feel victory is impossible. But each of these passages shows Satan can be beaten. (More about that in chapter 7.)

Finally, we learn that all victories over Satan are but temporary. He will come back and try again. This is discouraging, but it's important for you to realize it. Satan left Jesus only for a while. Later he came back. You can expect no less for yourself. But many people think that once they gain victory over a bad habit, they are secure for life. Not so! Satan will return, and you need to anticipate and prepare for that occasion.

Satan's persistence surprised a godly professor of mine when I was in college. He walked into our class one day with a disturbed look on his face. Unlike many, he felt no need to hide his failures from us, so he told us about what had just happened. He had handed back a mid-term exam to a freshman Bible survey class. The questioning became heated as the students reacted to the test, and he eventually lost his temper in answering them. With astonishment he related, "I thought I had that problem taken care of years ago." But Satan in his wiliness had slipped in where the professor thought he had victory.

Satan Challenges God's Truth

The serpent was the craftiest of all the creatures the Lord God had made. So the serpent came to the woman. "Really?" he asked. "*None* of the fruit in the garden? God says you mustn't eat any of it?"

"Of course we may eat it," the woman told him. "It's

only the fruit from the tree at the *center* of the garden that we are not to eat. God says we mustn't eat it or even touch it, or we will die."

"That's a lie!" the serpent hissed. "You'll not die! God knows very well that the instant you eat it you will become like Him, for your eyes will be opened — you will be able to distinguish good from evil!"

The woman was convinced. How lovely and fresh looking it was! And it would make her so wise! So she ate some of the fruit and gave some to her husband, and he ate it too. And as they ate it, suddenly they became aware of their nakedness, and were embarrassed. So they strung fig leaves together to cover themselves around the hips. (Gen. 3:1-7)

Satan challenges the truthfulness of God's Word as a means of tempting you. At times in response, you probably distort God's Word also. You need to recognize this as a key battleground in your thought life. You must let God's Word speak plainly to you under the Spirit's guidance. You must beware of the temptation to distort His Word to justify actions you know are wrong. We can see how far this can go in 1 Corinthians 5, where Paul found it necessary to rebuke the church for permitting one of its members to live with his stepmother in an immoral relationship, a relationship they justified by reference to their freedom in Christ.

Modern Christians also twist Scripture to justify what they know is wrong. A minister acquaintance became involved with a woman in his church. She originally came to him for counseling, but as the relationship developed, they fell in love with one another and entered an affair. As the problems growing from the affair grew more and more complex, the pastor sought counsel. As he revealed his problem, his lack of perspective became clear. He stated, "I've been praying that God would keep people from finding out what I'm doing, because I don't want to hurt my ministry." He had become convinced that the problem lay not in what he was doing but in discovery. Such is the subtle power of Satan to assist us in twisting God's Word to justify our actions, actions we would condemn in others.

Genesis 3 also teaches that Adam yielded to temptation as a result of pressure from his wife. The pressure was subtle, for she neither forced him to eat nor nagged him for not eating. She simply offered him the fruit. Her very presence and offer, however, constituted strong pressure to eat. Similarly, social pressure, particularly from those close to us, is one of the major forces that destroys our resistance to temptation. We all like to please others. As a result, we try to do what others want of us. Thus, social pressure often helps maintain our bad habits.

Sharon learned this the hard way. As she came into counseling, I could see she was depressed. We had been working for about a month on her weight problem, and she felt good about her progress. The previous Friday, however, she had blown her diet to pieces. A former college roommate had come into town and asked her out to dinner. She hadn't seen Dorothy in almost ten years. They went out to a favorite eating spot and had a large meal. They followed this with a trip to a favorite ice cream parlor for dessert. If it hadn't been for Dorothy's visit, Sharon thinks she might have stayed with her weight reduction program. In our continuing work together, though, Sharon learned how to deal with social pressures such as this situation illustrates.

God Offers Wisdom

> If you want to know what God wants you to do, ask him, and he will gladly tell you, for he is always ready to give a bountiful supply of wisdom to all who ask him; he will not resent it. (James 1:5)

Here we learn that to face temptation effectively, you have to admit you need God's wisdom. Too often we seek to fight temptation in our own strength and wisdom. Then when we fail we blame God. But James reminds us that as soon as you admit your need, God is there ready to work on your behalf.

I learned this in helping a friend with a problem we shared. Betty and I stood talking in the church narthex when Caroline walked through the door. She greeted us and walked on into the church office. After she left, Betty looked at me and said, "Seeing that woman makes me think, what can I do to overcome a critical spirit? Each time I see her, all I can think about are criticisms."

My first response was, "You'll just have to learn to use it in a good way." I, too, had dealt with a critical spirit for years. But then God began to work and show me His wisdom. He helped me see that I could use my critical powers to spot areas in others' lives where they needed my prayers. He also showed me that I could use my critical powers to observe areas where others needed help and then see if I couldn't find ways of assisting without being pushy. The solution was so simple once I began to seek God's wisdom through another's request.

Thus, you should also expect God to guide you in your battle by giving you wisdom. My hope is that throughout this book you will be helped to gain some of that wisdom under the Holy Spirit's guidance. You will develop a plan of attack specifically directed toward your needs. You will gain victory over your bad habit as God gives you wisdom to fight the battle.

Assignment:

1. List the eleven principles of temptation given in this chapter.

   1 Corinthians 10:13:
      A.
      B.
      C.

   Mathew 4:1-11 and Hebrews 4:15:
      A.
      B.
      C.
      D.
      E.

   Genesis 3:1-7:
      A.
      B.

   James 1:5:
      A.

2. Memorize 1 Corinthians 10:13, and think about it when you face temptation.

Further Reading:

Dietrich Bonhoeffer, *Creation and Fall: Temptation* (Macmillan).
Charles R. Swindoll, *Three Steps Forward, Two Steps Back* (Nashville: Thomas Nelson)

7

Resisting Satan

Have you ever carried on a conversation with Satan? If you're like most people, the idea has never crossed your mind. You might even find it a little frightening. That's how I felt when I first ran across the idea. The very thought also made me feel foolish. Eventually I learned, however, that talking to Satan is a key element in the battle plan against temptation.

Submission to God and His will are your primary means of combating temptation. You cannot regularly resist God and expect to win your battles with temptation. In fact, one of the most important elements in your battle with temptation is simply a close walk with God. You need to combine periodic resistance to the devil, however, with your submission to God. James wrote, "So give yourselves humbly to God. Resist the devil and he will flee from you" (4:7). When he comes with his temptations, you need to know how to meet him.

Your mind is a battleground where Satan and God fight. The outcome is certain so long as you submit to God and resist the devil. Paul said, "Don't you realize that you can choose your own master? You can choose sin (with death) or else obedience (with acquittal). The one to whom you offer yourself — he will take you and be your master and you will be his slave" (Rom. 6:16). The key element in all of this is your will. The side you favor at any given moment will begin to win. The longer you support one side, the greater its strength becomes in overcoming the other. Thus, your will determines who will be victorious.

The battleground for temptation, then, is your mind. To a certain extent this was already suggested in the earlier chapters on your thought life. This is such a specialized aspect of the thought life, however, that it needs concentrated attention. If habits come from actions and actions derive from thoughts, then stopping Satan in his attacks at the level of your thoughts will make victory easier.

However, as we look at this battle plan against Satan, a note of caution is in order. This plan works best against what I call persistent or obsessive types of temptation. For example, I don't think knuckle cracking or fingernail biting fall into these categories. You rarely become obsessed with the idea of cracking your knuckles or biting your fingernails. On the other hand, worry, anger, unclean thoughts, bitterness, and many other habits do fall into this category. At times, worry can be so persistent that you will be unable to drive it from your mind. Anger can control you to the extent that you will wonder if you have any command of yourself. Bitter thoughts can crowd your mind, preventing you from ministering to others. Unclean thoughts can drive you to distraction. These persistent, obsessive types of temptation respond best to the method presented in this chapter.

Know Your Enemy

Before describing the plan, however, there are a number of other things with which we need to deal. I recently read an Old West novel in which an Indian was hurt by some white men. He followed them, seeking revenge. But when he caught up with them, he didn't attack immediately. Instead, he spent almost a week watching them to see how they lived. He reasoned, *Since they have superior force and numbers, the better I know them, the more chance my attack will be successful.* In your battle against Satan, the more you know about him, the better your chances for success.

Satan is a real person, just as real as Jesus Christ. Because we live in a world that focuses on material values and material living, we often have a hard time accepting the reality of things we cannot see. Particularly when our world considers people foolish who acknowledge the reality of a living, personal devil. Many people have a hard time believing Satan exists. But he is real. He even talked with Jesus on at least one occasion when

He was on this earth, as we just saw.

The devil's reality, however, should not cause you to be afraid of him. We can agree that he is one of God's highest created beings (Isa. 14:12-17), but he is not a person we should fear unreasonably.

I first became conscious of this unjustified fear when I was a student at Taylor University and a missionary joined us for one of our annual missions conferences. As a missionary to the Philippines, he had dealt firsthand with demonism and Satan worship. Students began asking questions in these areas. At first he resisted talking about the subject, but eventually he gave in. His method of giving in, however, set a frightening stage. He said, "I greatly dislike talking about this subject, but if you insist I will talk with you about it. First, however, let's all spend a period of time in prayer for protection from Satan's devices during and after our discussion." While I now appreciate his concern, having dealt with these matters personally, I think he needlessly frightened many of us.

Because he is a defeated enemy, Satan should not frighten us. He is limited by God's power. In Job 1:12 and 2:6, God specifically limited what Satan was permitted to do to Job, showing how He limits his activity in all our lives. "And the Lord replied to Satan, 'You may do anything you like with his [Job's] wealth, but don't harm him physically'....'Do with him as you please,' the Lord replied, 'only spare his life.' "
Through the cross of Jesus Christ, Satan has already been defeated. John told his readers, "But the Son of God came to destroy these works of the devil" (1 John 3:8b). Although you should still respect him in his battles for control of your mind and life, you need not fear him, because he is defeated. By using (in faith) the name of Jesus Christ, you can overcome him.

Who is Satan? He is given many names in the Bible, but above all he is the king of deceivers. Jesus called him "the father of liars" (John 8:44). Peter told us, "Be careful — watch out for attacks from Satan, your great enemy. He prowls around like a hungry, roaring lion, looking for some victim to tear apart" (1 Pet. 5:8). Yet he deceives by making himself appear to be an angel of light. Paul said in 2 Corinthians 11:14-15, "Satan can change himself into an angel of light, so it is no wonder his servants can do it too, and seem like godly ministers." That is, he distorts normal human values. He makes wrong look right and right appear wrong in his attempts to mess up human thinking. You need to be constantly aware of this tendency on his part.

He makes his appeals in a number of ways. His most effective appeal is to your old nature. Before conversion, you sinned. The memory of your sins lies hidden in the recesses of your mind. Satan brings those memories to the surface as the foundation for a new temptation. In fact, he often uses the pleasures of old sin to entice you into another taste of the same sin. (This is why it is so necessary to deal with past guilt as a means of breaking a bad habit, as will be discussed in chapter 9.)

Don was talking with one of the church board members about the pull of former sins. Joe commented, "I became a Christian as a child. I sometimes think I missed out on a lot by not getting involved in some of the pleasures of the world before I became a Christian."

Don responded, "Don't believe it. Satan constantly uses my old sins to tempt me. I would give all I have to be freed from the memory of some of the things I did before I became a Christian."

Satan makes another appeal through your natural appetites and desires. Israel's downfall came time and again through intermarriage. Look at most sins. What are they? They are largely a natural appetite taken too far. You get fat because you eat too much, but the desire to eat keeps you from starving to death. Satan uses this elemental desire to get you into trouble.

David fell because he was attracted to Bathsheba's beauty, but male-female attraction is essential for the survival of the human race.

Darrold was a particularly sharp Christian in our church, and he was always on the lookout for ways of helping others. He discovered that Alice, a young divorcee down the street, was having a hard time keeping up her home. He assisted with first one thing and then another. Before either of them knew what was happening, they were involved in an affair. Darrold's desire to help got out of control. Thus Satan takes normal desires and uses them to destroy lives.

How does he do this? Satan attacks through your thought life. Satan, like God, is a spiritual being who has no body. That means he cannot talk to you as a human being would. But you also have a spiritual nature. Satan communicates to you mind to mind, even as the Holy Spirit does. He plants suggestions. He makes you sensitive to events that might appeal to you. Your later actions and habits that we call sin result from Satan's initial appeal in your mind. This is the original sensitivity training. You become sensitized to elements in your environment that will lead you into sin.

As the father of liars, Satan is very subtle in his attacks. When he approached Jesus in Matthew 4:1-11, he never said to Jesus directly, "Turn Your back on God and serve me." No, he is not that foolish. He appealed to Jesus' natural appetites and desires. The message behind his words was, "Make bread and feed Yourself, since You're hungry"; "Make people listen to You by doing something spectacular, since You have such an important mission"; "Win the world to Your cause, as God wants You to, by worshipping me." So subtle, so devious. This is his method. He always gives you justification for your sinning. That is why I asked you earlier to examine your own rationalizations. When they are brought into the light of day, you can see the prince of darkness for who he is.

Satan is particularly subtle in the way he uses God's Word. Yes, Satan often uses God's Word in his temptations. Two of Jesus' temptations contain quotations from the Old Testament. When Satan tempted Eve in the garden of Eden, he intentionally distorted God's Word to trap her. You must be particularly careful if, when you are struggling with temptation, a verse from the Bible appears to justify what you used to think was sin. Satan uses God's Word — in distorted form — to tempt you, because he knows how highly you regard the Bible.

Know Yourself

While knowing your enemy is a key element in winning any battle, knowing yourself is also important. If you do not know your own strengths and weaknesses, you may fail because you try something you cannot handle. You need to be particularly sensitive to temptations in your areas of weakness. Samson fell in major ways in two different encounters with women, but he kept playing with temptation until he met Delilah and, as a result of not facing his weakness, he lost his standing with God.

Dave was startled by his weakness for cigarettes. Work was finished for the day, but dismissal bell had not rung. We all gathered in the corner of our work area to talk. The rules in our area absolutely prohibited smoking because it was a fire hazard. As we talked Dave suddenly exclaimed, "Where did this thing come from?" In his hand was a cigarette he had lit while talking with us. He didn't have even the slightest idea of what he had done. Because many habits are like that, you need to sensitize yourself to the signs that you are moving toward engaging in your habit, asking the Holy Spirit to help you see what is happening before it is too late.

Part of sensitizing yourself is learning all you can about your habit. Another part should be to ask the Holy Spirit for the wisdom to see what you are doing. James 1:5, which we looked at earlier, is also helpful here. It has particular application to your temptations. You need God's wisdom in order to become sensitive enough to recognize what you are doing.

Harry was totally unaware of his offensive language. When I worked for a security firm in Chicago, Harry, who was my staff sergeant, swore worse than any person I've ever met. Yet we worked constantly with people in business who did not like that kind of language. The boss reprimanded him time and again. It wasn't that Harry was trying to be disobedient. He honestly didn't know it when he was swearing. Only as you become sensitive to all aspects of your temptation will you win your battles with Satan.

Satan's most effective attacks come after he has lulled you into complacency. Paul warned us, "So be careful. If you are thinking 'Oh, I would never behave like that' — let this be a warning to you. For you too may fall into sin" (1 Cor. 10:12). Satan waits for moments when you are not watchful. As a former security guard, I know that the biggest advantage a criminal has is his state of alertness. Guards easily become complacent because they spend days, weeks, months and even years without ever facing a crisis. The criminal is alert for trouble, while the guard is at ease. Satan also attacks best when you're off guard. Thus, you need to be always on the alert for his attacks, as Peter warned (1 Pet. 5:8).

Jeff came into my office with a hang-dog expression on his face. About a week earlier, he had come back from a business trip during which he had encountered a subtle temptation which caught him napping. As a youth traveling back and forth between college, he got into the habit of reading pornographic literature in the bus stations. After college he gained victory over this, but when he went on this recent trip, he got caught with a four-hour layover in Chicago's O'Hare Airport. As he looked for something to occupy him during that time, he wandered through the newsstand area. Soon he found himself engrossed in the pornography he found there, but he left deeply disturbed at his fall. Satan had caught him unaware, just as he did David with Bathsheba.

Resisting Satan

Now for our battle plan. The key element in resisting Satan is a planned conversation with him. The pattern for this conversation comes from Jesus' temptation in Matthew 4:1-11. Each time Satan attacked, Jesus responded by addressing him, "The Bible says...," and then He quoted an appropriate passage. Because you are not Jesus Christ but are only acting with His authority (Matt. 28:18-20), you should add one element to that approach. Whatever you say to Satan should be said in the name of Jesus Christ. Our pattern of resisting Satan, then, goes like this:

> Satan, in the name and by the authority of Jesus Christ go away, because the Bible, God's Word, says [whatever passage applies to your temptation].

You call Satan by name simply because he is a person with a name and that is the most natural way to address him.

You address him in the name of Jesus Christ because in your own strength or name you have no power over him. He can easily defeat you if you approach him in your own power. See what happened to the sons of Sceva in Acts 19:13-16, when they rebuked Satan in their own power. So you use Jesus' name because we are God's children, and we have victory over Satan through the cross of Jesus Christ.

Finally, you use the Word of God, the Bible, against Satan because God's Word is the only offensive weapon in the Christian's arsenal. Ephesians 6:17 tells us, "You will need the helmet of salvation and the sword of the Spirit — which is the Word of God." It is designed to keep us from sin. "I have thought much about your words, and stored them in my heart so that they would hold me back from sin," said the psalmist as he meditated on God's Word (Ps. 119:11).

You don't have to be afraid to talk with Satan in this way, because he already has been defeated by Jesus Christ, as John told us: "The Son of God came to destroy these works of the devil" (1 John 3:8c). You are not being disrespectful; you are using the offensive weapon God gave us for our battles with Satan. You have nothing to fear at this point except the disabling effects of fear itself.

Potential Problems

Do you feel foolish thinking about talking to Satan? I did. Part of this goes back to our involvement in a material world in which those who talk with nonmaterial beings are considered nuts. So be it. We may be considered nuts, but let's use the tools God has given us.

When I first talked to Satan, I sat quietly in my office even though inwardly I was tremendously frustrated. I had been trying for most of the morning to prepare my sermon for Sunday, but I would hardly get started when my mind would be barraged by unclean thoughts. I prayed, asking God to take the thoughts away. As soon as I started back to work, they came again. This procedure had gone on for some time when I began to think, What would happen if after I prayed I also told Satan in Jesus' name to leave me alone? I felt foolish even thinking about it. But again the unclean thoughts filled my mind. Finding I had no other choice, I began my short conversation with Satan. Then I went back to work. Suddenly it dawned on me. I had been working for more than an hour without a single unclean thought. It worked! But did I ever feel foolish talking to Satan! Not until I had used this method on numerous occasions did I really feel comfortable with it. All feelings of foolishness eventually disappeared.

You cannot stop, however, with a conversation with Satan. When Satan leaves, he leaves behind him an empty space. Jesus told the disciples in Luke 11:24-26,

> When a demon is cast out of a man, it goes to the deserts, searching there for rest; but finding none, it returns to the person it left, and finds that its former home is all swept and clean. Then it goes and gets seven other demons more evil than itself, and they all enter the man. And so the poor fellow is seven times worse off than he was before.

A basic law of nature is that empty spaces get filled. If you don't have something to put into your mind as soon as Satan leaves, he will soon return. Finding his recently vacated home so nicely cleaned, he will invite a few friends to join him.

To avoid this danger, you need to plan things you can do or think about as soon as Satan is gone. My suggestion is to think about a passage of Scripture. Begin to let the verse run around in your mind. Ask yourself questions about how it applies in your life. What can you do to implement it? As you think on these things, you will fill your mind with the words of God, thus keeping Satan at bay for a longer period of time. God's Word, both as a sword in conflict and as a means of changing your thought life, is a crucial tool for keeping Satan from gaining access to your mind.

Assignment:

1. Memorize Psalm 119:9,11.
1. Write out the pattern for a conversation with Satan on a small card. Carry it with you so you can have it handy whenever you need to use it.
3. Write out a paragraph of your own describing Satan.

Further reading:

Bill Bright, *The Holy Spirit* (Here's Life Publishers), chapters 11-14.

"Satan" in *New Bible Dictionary* (Eerdmans).

8

The Nature of Your Temptation

Your temptation is uniquely and peculiarly yours. No one else has a temptation precisely like yours.

I imagine right now you are saying, "Hold it. Didn't you say earlier that all our temptations are common to people? Didn't you say that no one ever has a unique temptation?" Yes, I did. Let's see if I can put these statements together so they make sense.

All temptations are common to humanity. Over the years, Satan has developed a bag of tricks so effective that he doesn't need to create anything new to get you. He knows everything about people's needs and how he can use them as the basis for temptation.

Nonetheless, each person is unique. The combination of your needs and desires is uniquely yours, even though all the individual desires are common to humanity. When we look at temptation, therefore, we do not want to limit ourselves by looking only at temptation in general.

As a result, you need to examine your temptation in minute detail so that you can describe precisely what it is. All of this is *preparation* for your battle to break your bad habit.

The Big Picture

You need a detailed picture of your habit from start to finish. If you're like most of us, you view your bad habits in isolation from the rest of your life. As a result, you often fail to see the events leading up to the habit and the relief your habit brings.

Part of breaking a bad habit, however, means learning to control thoughts and feelings that precede the habit. You may also have to create negative results (punishment) following your habit so that it is no longer satisfying. Because your habit meets a need, you must also learn which need it is so that you can develop alternative ways of satisfying it.

Thus, *before* you can actually begin work on breaking a bad habit, you need an accurate picture of the habit and the events, people, and times surrounding your failures. When you complete this picture, you will be in a stronger position to overcome the habit.

Samson illustrates the results of failure to understand this dynamic. He is a tragic hero in the book of Judges. His habit was romantic relationships with non-Christian women. He fell into his habit by walking through the countryside observing pagan women instead of looking only at Israelite women, women God approved. He seemed to find enjoyment in "playing with fire," so he constantly challenged situations with these women until at last me met his downfall in Delilah. His habit included far more than simply relationships with women forbidden by God, however. It began with tantalizing looks and the excitement of playing with danger.

Joan thought her problem was that she was not able to keep a clean house. She struggled to keep a clean house, but the most difficult area was the kitchen. On more than one occasion, the pile of dishes was so high that her mother-in-law actually used a visit simply to wash dishes for her. Joan felt humiliated, but she just couldn't motivate herself to wash dishes until they were out of just about everything. As we discussed her habit, we began to expand our search for causes.

At first Joan saw nothing more than the growing pile of dishes. But as we examined her self-talk, we discovered that she felt she was unfairly burdened by the rest of the family. No one else helped with any of the housework, and they simply scattered dishes not only in the kitchen but throughout the house, leaving them wherever they were when they finished using them. Joan found that she was telling herself, *This isn't fair. I shouldn't have to trail them throughout the house looking for dishes.* She also discovered she resented their complaining about the dirty dishes when often, since her children were teenagers, they could have taken a minute and cleaned what they needed. She also discovered, though, that she enjoyed their complaining even as she was hating it. It was her revenge for having to clean up after them. In all of this she discovered, as you ought, that habits are bigger than most people think.

As you create a detailed picture of your habit, you will also begin to discover why you have it. Remember, we only keep habits because they meet our needs. People often have problems breaking a habit because they don't know what need it meets. Once they learn that, they can create alternative ways of satisfying the need, ways that are more acceptable to themselves, society, and God. As He invites in James 1:5, seek His wisdom to accurately describe your habit.

Description

Let's create a detailed picture of your habit. Take a sheet of paper and write out a complete description of your habit. I will use my own bad habit of anger as an example.

Something happens that I don't like. Generally this means someone makes me put up with something I don't like, or they refuse to do something I want them to do. I don't immediately show my anger. I generally stuff it down inside so they won't see I'm angry. But I can tell I'm angry because I begin to speak more softly, I carefully measure my words, and I may even have difficulty speaking because I'm afraid of what will happen if I let people know I'm angry. Then I brood over this offense. As I brood, I tend to magnify its size. In doing this, I fail to see the other person's point of view and usually exaggerate my own rights. By this time, I'm at the point where my anger may come out in public. If it does, I will speak sharply to the person, often including an insult for good measure. If the person chooses to argue with me, I will insist on my own perspective and have little toleration for any other. When it is all finished, I will probably brood over the event again, possibly for a number of days, until at last I settle down.

Now I want you to write a similarly detailed description of your bad habit. To aid you, let me suggest a number of points you should consider.

The Beginning

Begin by writing out the thoughts or actions that precede your temptation or bad habit. For example, when I get angry, one of the first thoughts that goes through my mind is, *They can't do that to me.* I might not actually say it to myself, but as I look back on my anger, that is frequently a part of it. I also usually think, *This is not right. I'll show them how wrong they are.* I then spend a period of time stewing over what has happened. I also slowly convince myself that the person who "wronged" me needs to be told. There are my thoughts. My actions include, as I related earlier, speaking more quietly, carefully weighing my words, and sometimes speaking so carefully that I can hardly talk because I'm holding my breath and my vocal cords are tight with tension.

Who? What? Where?

Second, identify situations, activities, and people associated with your bad habit. All of Jacob's schemes involved conflict with family members and his need to accumulate more wealth than they had.

Chris had a problem that was creating difficulties for his Christian witness. He always had to tell a better story than the other guy. As I spoke with him about the impression this left on others, he said, "But I can't seem to help myself. I get into a situation determined to sit and listen, but when people begin talking, I suddenly hear myself telling a 'better' story. I don't like it, but I can't seem to stop it." We went to work examining the who, what and where of his problem. We soon discovered that he only had to be better than others with whom he felt insecure. If the "who" was someone he wanted to impress, or the "where" a situation in which he felt he had to make an impact, then he began bragging again. The "what" was simply situations of casual conversation.

So write out your situations, activities, and the people associated with your bad habit. This will help you get a picture of what is happening at the time you fail.

Hiding

Now write out those things you do to conceal your habit from others. As you go through this process, some items will overlap with others. That's all right. We want as full and detailed a picture of your habit as you can create. It's only by knowing everything you can about your habit that you can gain victory over it.

Jonah displayed a common reaction to anger. He hid it by running away. He withdrew, first by fleeing to Tarshish in the ship as a means of not having to confront God with his anger, and then by sitting outside Nineveh and pouting when things didn't go his way. But in each instance he withdrew rather than face the cause of his anger.

Franz had the habit of saying yes to every request made of him and then hiding it from others. This meant he never had enough time for family and was always too busy to do the things his wife needed help with around the house. When they came in for counseling, her complaint was not so much his habit as the way he handled it. When he accepted a new responsibility, he wouldn't say anything about it. Then at the last minute, when nothing could be done, he would spring it on her and walk out the door to his new assignment. His failure to mention the new responsibility neatly hid it until nothing more could be done.

Now write out the things you do to conceal your habit.

Excuses

How do you rationalize your habit? That is, how do you justify doing what you know you shouldn't? May is a procrastinator. No matter what job she has, she never seems to get it done until at least two minutes after the deadline, and often long after it. But something always seems to happen, according to her story, that keeps her from getting things done on time. The kids need help with something else; she gets an unexpected phone call; the car breaks down; her husband asks her to run some errands. The excuses vary, but the theme is always the same: "Well, I could have been done on time if I hadn't been interrupted with . . ."

Write out what you do or think that justifies continuing your habit.

Needs

Next, ask yourself what need or needs your habit is meeting. Every habit meets a need. Habits that continue when you would like to break them usually meet a significant need. Thus, you need to discover what that need is so that you can plan a more effective way of meeting it.

As Roland and I talked about his apparent need to control every conversation, we sought a need his talking might meet. At first nothing seemed to show up, but then he commented, "You know, I think I want to be liked by everybody, and I'm convinced they'll like me if I always have a good story to tell." This discovery led to a more relaxed atmosphere as he saw the foolishness of trying to have everyone like him, an impossible task for anyone.

Charting

At this point, I want you to monitor your habit for a week as a way of discovering the above information and putting it together as a habit picture. To do this, create a chart like the following on 3" x 5" cards that you will carry around with you:

```
PERSON:
EVENT:
DAY:
TIME:
THOUGHTS:
EMOTIONS:
SITUATION:
```

Each time you encounter your habit, chart what time your habit occurs and also on what day. Write down the incident or incidents (event) that led to the habit — that is, those that immediately preceded it. In addition, write down any people who were around who might have had an influence on the way you acted. Also write down your emotional state. Write down the thoughts going through your mind at the time. Then describe the general situation.

This chart will expose key situations in which you are

particularly susceptible to temptation. It will also give you a glimpse of other aspects of your temptation that you need to know.

After you complete the chart, analyze it. Look for any pattern that comes to your mind that says, *This is the time, situation, or person involved when I am prone to fail.* If Samson were doing this, he would have noted that he always fell when walking through the countryside observing Philistine women and thinking about how challenging and nice it would be to have one of them.

Marge discovered another pattern. As I worked with her over a period of a year to control her promiscuous behavior, we discovered a pattern that explained what was happening. She had been divorced for almost six years. Her former husband, Ken, had for all practical purposes abandoned the children. But every few months, he either called or visited with no advance warning. By the time he left, the kids were upset, and it would take a few days for them to get back to normal behavior. Marge struggled at all times with loneliness, but after Ken visited, the loneliness, the disruptive behavior from the kids, and her own trapped feelings got to be too much. She would respond with relief to an invitation to go out for the evening, and before it was over she would find herself in bed with her date. She didn't want to do it, but it kept happening. Insight into the pattern that led to her behavior gave a basis for planning ways to gain victory over it.

As you analyze your own chart at the end of a week, see what patterns you can discover that indicate times, situations, or people that make you particularly vulnerable. (If charting for a week doesn't help, you may need more time, just as Marge did.)

Habit Picture

Write out a detailed description of your habit.
1. Thoughts or actions that precede my habit.
2. Who's around? What am I doing? Where am I?
3. Ways I conceal my habit.
4. Excuses that justify my habit.
5. What needs does my habit meet?

Our purpose in this chapter has been to create a detailed description of your habit. Only you can describe your habit in a way that will eventually help you break it. Only you know what you do, and the events leading up to your habit. This is why I want you to spend a week figuring out what your habit involves. You also need to do this *before* you attempt to break your habit. If you don't know what precedes the habit, you will put the brakes on too late to be effective. If you don't recognize your rationalizing behavior for what it is, you will believe false information and continue your habit. For these and other reasons emphasized in this book, complete this description of your habit before you make any attempt to break it. Until you know your habit well, better than you ever have in the past, you will have difficulty in breaking it. You need this analysis to lay a foundation for your coming victory. Since this is both an important and difficult task (because the human heart is so deceitful), you particularly need to seek the Holy Spirit's assistance in writing the description. So your assignment for this coming week is to create a detailed picture of your habit using charting and the habit picture.

Assignment:

1. Ask God for wisdom as you do steps 2 - 4.
2. Chart your habit on 3" x 5" cards for seven days (longer if it is an infrequent habit).
3. Write out any pattern you see after finishing your charting.
4. Complete your own habit picture.

9

The Burden of Guilt

Louise decided to surprise Eric by losing weight while he was out of town at a two-week business seminar learning new computer techniques. She began her diet the day he left. The first few days went fine, but she discovered that the evenings were long and empty with him gone. Once the children were in bed, she sat and watched TV, but it seemed that every commercial pointed toward food. She resisted with all her will, but finally she walked into the kitchen one evening and snacked on the cake she gave the kids for dessert. Having taken her first bite, she said to herself, *Ah, you can't keep away from this sweet stuff anyhow. You might as well just give up.* By the time she was finished, she had eaten half the cake and her diet was gone. During the next few days she gorged herself out of pity at falling off her diet.

Afraid to Try

Many bad habits continue as a response to guilt. See if the following description rings true with you. Whenever you engage in a bad habit, you feel bad. You repeat it, however, because you feel you are so bad that there is simply no use in trying. At the same time, your guilt keeps you from resisting. It smothers your motivation to change. Having tried and constantly failed you begin to say to yourself, *I'm so bad, what's the use in trying again?* You pound yourself into the ground with guilt feelings that make you even more prone to fall into your favorite sins.

I'm reminded of an experiment done a few years ago with

northern pike. Northern pike are particularly vicious fresh water fish that attack their prey like a lion pouncing on a gazelle. Experimenters put a northern pike in a large aquarium. The first few days they dropped minnows into the aquarium for the pike to eat. After a few days of this, they slipped a glass partition down the middle of the tank. A short time later, they released the minnows on the opposite side of the barrier. The pike looked at the minnows for a few moments and then charged, smashing his nose against the glass. He backed off, puzzled. A few minutes later he tried again. He only hurt his nose.

This behavior continued for a while until the pike got accustomed to the minnows swimming in the same water with him, but on the other side of the barrier. After a few days of this, the experimenters removed the barrier. Now the minnows could swim anywhere they wanted, but so could the pike. The smaller fishes' lives appeared to be in danger. But nothing happened. One of the minnows actually bumped into the pike's nose without getting a response. He "knew" that the moment he tried to get that minnow, he was going to hurt his nose. Eventually he had to be taken from the aquarium and placed in a new environment to keep him from starving.

Many people, as a result of past failure, lose all motivation to break their bad habits. It's not that they haven't tried. The problem is they have tried so often — they have gotten their hopes so high and they have been hurt so badly when they failed — that they don't want to try again. Almost nothing can give them the motivation they need to try once more. I hope the plan in this book will encourage you to make another attempt.

What often complicates this is that you get angry at yourself for failing. Anger is a very common response to guilt. However, many habits are also continuing responses to anger in your life, at least in part. Thus, your guilt combines with anger about your guilt to make breaking your habit even more difficult.

Larry demonstrated this mixture of anger and guilt as he struggled to bring his masturbation under control. He felt guilty because he regularly masturbated, but he was also deeply angry with himself for his inability to control himself. He learned to deal with his anger by recognizing that no one controls a major habit in a single day. On the other hand, he learned to deal with his guilt through the principles given in this chapter.

Forgiven by God

What can you do, then, with this guilt that has so sapped you that you have almost given up hope? The best cure for guilt is a clear conscience. You have to seek forgiveness from God and others. Finally, and most difficult, you have to seek forgiveness from yourself.

First, you need to seek forgiveness from God. You need to confess your failure to Him, just as it says in 1 John 1:9, and ask Him to forgive you for hurting Him, for hurting others, and for hurting yourself by your sin. You should confess your sin in all the detail we discovered in the last chapter. Often we do not feel forgiven by God because we take our sin too lightly, even though we may anguish over it. Or we have seen our sin as far smaller than it really is. If we can see the extent of our sin, it makes it easier to appreciate God's forgiveness.

When David sinned by committing adultery with Bathsheba and then having her husband killed, he felt guilty and remorseful about failing God. However, he didn't feel sufficiently remorseful to act as he should have until the prophet Nathan challenged him with the seriousness of his sin. An exercise such as we did in the last chapter can help you to see how serious your sin really is.

But we also need to deal with this problem of "sensing God's forgiveness." God promises that when you confess your sin, He faithfully forgives your sin, just as He has promised (1 John 1:9). You need to cling to that fact once you've confessed your sin, no matter how you feel. You are forgiven whether you feel forgiven or not. However, when you're dealing with a longstanding problem, there is value in a time with God in which you reveal the depth of your hurt, concern, and remorse and seek His forgiveness, clinging to the fact of His promise while still realizing the special sense of wholeness that often comes with forgiveness.

How often can you come to Him for this forgiveness? Does

a time come when He gets disgusted and says to you, "Oh, it's you again. Won't you ever stop this childish behavior and live the way I want you to?" Thank God, He is never that way. You can come as often as you sin. God wants you to desire change and to make an effort to change. But He knows far better than we do that perfection is reserved for heaven. He knows you may fail hundreds of times before you finally succeed, but He loves you just as much when you fail as He does when you succeed. He refills you with His Holy Spirit each time you ask for forgiveness and a new filling.

Probably no failure stands out more than Peter's denial of Jesus. Here was a man who walked closely with Jesus for three years. Yet when Jesus most needed his support, he not only fled, but when challenged about his relationship with Christ, he even denied he ever knew Him. After the resurrection, however, Jesus specially sought Peter out and drew him back to Himself at the seashore. He never once condemned Peter for his failure. Instead, Christ asked Peter whether he was still willing to follow Him. Similarly with you, He's not nearly so concerned about your past failure as He is about your present willingness to try again

If we only realized it, we regularly treat others this way. I manage a Little League baseball team during the summer. I see many failures by my team of boys 10-13 years old. They occasionally make horrendous blunders in areas we've discussed in the past. But once the mistake is made, my concern as a manager is not to tear them down but to encourage them to try again so they can do better in the future. This is the way God treats us as we try to change.

Sometimes, however, your confession to God needs to be supplemented by confession to God in the presence of a mature Christian friend. I don't know why, but many times we cannot feel forgiven until we have asked a friend to pray with us about our sin. Theologically, God forgives us when we ask Him. He doesn't need a friend with us when we pray. But with habits that have a strong hold over our lives, particularly habits that shame or embarrass us (such as sexual immorality), having a friend with us when we pray seems to make a difference.

Suzanne discovered this as we worked through what she thought was an unusual problem. She grew up in a family in which her mother was either demon possessed or seriously mentally ill, but not enough so that she was ever hospitalized. During Suzanne's childhood, she was brutalized as her mother mocked everything she did, constantly belittling her. Even after she left home, her mother continued to harass her, spreading all sorts of lies about her and her new husband — on one occasion almost causing them to separate because of her gossiping. After Suzanne became a Christian, she continued to struggle with her relationship with her mother. One day I casually commented, "If I were in your shoes, I would hate my mother. Is that the way you feel?" It was like a dam burst. She had prayed time and again about this problem, but she never felt forgiven. After she discussed her hatred of her mother with me, however, the prayer that followed gave her freedom such as she'd never before known.

Forgiven by Others

We also often need to seek forgiveness from others for the hurt our habits have caused them, as Larry did. He came into the dining room one evening as the family sat down to dinner and said, "I want to tell you something. Over the past few years, I have set a bad example for you children and have caused many problems for you ... my wife, Wanda. I've wronged you by smoking, and I want to ask you to forgive me. Will you?"

This marked the beginning of the end of Larry's battle with cigarettes. There is something about confessing your sin to those you have hurt that gives backbone to your determination to change. Having confessed once, you don't want to put yourself in a position of having to confess again. As a result, you try harder in your effort to gain control.

Principles for Self-Forgiveness

1. God loves you even when you sin (Rom. 5:8, 8:33).
2. God gives you the freedom to fail when you're trying to change.
3. God does not try to control you with guilt or fear.
4. God's love frees you to try to change without fear of His rejection.

Now comes the tough part. How do you forgive yourself for the wrongs done as a result of your habit? First, begin by seeking God's forgiveness. Then seek others' forgiveness. We can't seem to forgive ourselves until we have first settled things with others. So begin with God and others.

Then remember what was said about the value of praying for forgiveness in the presence of a friend. Often a key indication of the need to seek God's forgiveness in the presence of a friend is the absence of a sense of forgiveness (even though you may know intellectually that God forgave your sin the moment you confessed it). When you just can't seem to forgive yourself for what you have done, you need to seek a mature Christian friend who can hear your prayer and reassure you of God's forgiveness.

I think even God realizes the need for this in dealing with serious sin. After Paul's conversion on the Damascus road, God sent Ananias to Paul to pray for him. When we consider all that Paul did during his pre-Christian experience, this demonstrates understanding on God's part. It's possible that without Ananias's assistance, Paul might always have felt unforgiven because his sins were so bad.

After you have done this, you need to concentrate your attention on God's love as revealed in Roman's 5:8: "But God showed His great love for us by sending Christ to die for us while we were still sinners." Here God says that He loved you before you came to Christ. In fact, while you were yet a rebellious sinner, He loved you. His love was so great that He sent His Son to die for your sins. But now you are His child. If His love was so great when you were His enemy how much greater His love must be now that you are His child! And if God loves you that much, how can you possibly not love yourself as His child?

What this means in practice is that you need to give yourself the freedom to fail while resting in God's love. Recognize that perfection is reserved for heaven and that God anticipates your failures. This is why He makes provision through verses like 1 John 1:9 for your continued forgiveness.

Having the freedom to fail while still maintaining my deep commitment to Jesus Christ has been one of the most liberating experiences of my life. As with many others, I've lived with a deep fear of failure, not only in my relationship with God, but also in my relationships with others and in my general approach to life. Then I slowly realized that God loves me just as much when I fail as He does when I succeed. That does not mean I take sin lightly, but it does mean I don't berate myself any longer when I fail. I simply turn to God, admit my failure, ask for a new filling with His Spirit, and go on with living. The freedom to fail is a wonderful freedom.

Our failures in no way diminish God's love for us. Many people have a hard time accepting this because our world, often the world of the families we grew up in, operates on different principles. When you were a child, your parents may have withheld love when you didn't do what they wanted. They gave what psychologists call *conditional love.* "You will be loved when you do what I want" is the message conveyed by this kind of love. "When you disobey, you will no longer be loved."

Now, however, you have entered a relationship with God as your heavenly Father and you as His child. But you still think (because you learned it as a child) that people in authority over you, such as parents, love you only when you do what they want. God, however, does not love that way. His love is unconditional. No matter what you do, He will continue to love you just as much as He ever has. He will be hurt by your offenses, but He will never stop loving you. Paul put it like this in Romans 8:38-39:

> For I am convinced that nothing can ever separate us from His love. Death can't, and life can't. The angels won't, and all the powers of hell itself cannot keep God's love away. Our fears for today, our worries about tomorrow, or where we are — high above the sky, or in the deepest ocean — nothing will ever be able to separate us from the love of God demonstrated by our Lord Jesus Christ when He died for us.

If He loves you to this extent, you can forgive yourself for what you have done wrong, just as He has.

Jesus did this with Peter after the crucifixion, when He dealt with his betrayal. Parents do it daily when their children fail them, yet they still love them deeply. You can be sure that God will always love you no matter what you do.

What most Christians fail to realize is that guilt is not a Christian emotion. That's right! Guilt is not a Christian emotion.

Guilt usually results when a person violates the law. It is not so much a feeling as it is a judgment. When you violate the law, you are guilty before the law.

As God's children, however, we no longer live under the law. The apostle Paul said, "We aren't saved from sin's grasp by knowing the commandments of God, because we can't and don't keep them, but God put into effect a different plan to save us. He sent His own Son in a human body like ours—except that ours are sinful—and destroyed sin's control over us by giving Himself as a sacrifice for our sins" (Rom. 8:3). It is not guilt but grace that provides the power to live the Christian life.

God does not want you to live your life free from sin because you are afraid of what He will do if you fail. God wants you to live a life freed from the fear of failure. The only way He can do that is to give you unconditional love that says, "No matter how badly you fail, I will still love you because My Son died to pay for your sins."

Without this unconditional love, you live in the fear of failure. But with this unconditional love, you have the freedom to try *and fail*. This is not because you want to fail, but because you know God loves you whether you are a failure or a success. (Bill Counts and Bruce Narramore develop this idea more fully in a book listed at the end of this chapter.)

All of this might not work for you. You seek God's forgiveness, you seek forgiveness from the people you hurt, and you seek self-forgiveness, but when you're done you still feel the burden of your sins. What should you do then? Some sins are overcome only through an extended period alone with God in prayer and fasting. While I do not have time to develop that idea here, Lorne Sanny of the Navigators has written an excellent booklet that can give you the help you need if you want to try praying and fasting as you seek assurance of forgiveness (see end of chapter).

All this means that you need to learn what Christian growth is all about. It involves the Holy Spirit at work within you, your responsibility to respond to the Spirit's work and love, and time to change.

The Holy Spirit works to accomplish His purpose with your

Elements of Christian Growth

1. The Holy Spirit is at work motivating and empowering you to change.
2. Your responsibility is to respond to the Spirit's directions.
3. You need time to change.

---

life. What is His purpose? He wants to reproduce the character of Jesus Christ in you, character represented by the fruit of the Spirit (Gal. 5:22-23).

The Holy Spirit then uses His methods to help you change. He does this by introducing experiences into your life that will help you change. Sometimes these are drastic, life-changing events, but at other times they are as simple as someone handing you a copy of this book and suggesting you use it.

A few years ago, God used a drastic method to help me. I've struggled most of my adult life with the need to impress people with who I am. This means I was unwilling to admit much in the way of weakness. It also meant I felt that I always had to succeed at anything I tried, no matter how difficult or unsuited to my personality. Then I lost my job as associate minister in a large church. The feeling was complete devastation. But from God's point of view, the changes were marvelous. The experience destroyed my fear of failure, because I had failed as badly as I could. It eliminated the need to impress others, because I learned you can't succeed at everything, so you should concentrate on what you do well. It also gave me much greater patience in dealing with others in their failures. Only the Holy Spirit could have accomplished these changes.

You also have a responsibility. The Holy Spirit is not going to change you while you are sitting in your recliner chair watching TV. He wants you to work at breaking your habits by His power within you. He also wants you to seek His will in determining which habits to work on when. The habits you choose should be those closely related to developing the fruit of the Spirit. So often there is a tendency to be trying to break a habit of overeating when God is saying, "You need to be more loving." Breaking habits involves selecting habits that will develop the fruit of the Spirit in your life.

Finally, you need to recognize that the Holy Spirit works in your life over a period of time. Paul says in Philippians 3:12 and Colossians 3:10,

> I don't mean to say I am perfect. I haven't learned all I should even yet, but I keep working toward that day when I will finally be all that Christ saved me for and wants me to be. . . . You are living a brand new kind of life that is continually learning more and more of what is right, and trying constantly to be more and more like Christ who created this new life within you.

Often when we read the lives of the great men and women of the Old Testament, we overlook the time factor. We marvel at how quickly Joseph went from being the proud little son of Jacob to being the ruler of Egypt. But when we look closely, we see that years went by while God taught Joseph humility. Howard Hendricks said in a meeting I attended, "One problem many young Christians face when they see older Christians is that they fail to realize the changes God has made over the years of their Christian lives. Older Christians need to share occasionally the road to God used to bring them to where they are now."

Time is also a factor in your life. Psychologists have discovered that people develop what is called a readiness to change or learn. The most common illustration of this is reading readiness. A child somewhere around the age of five or six develops a readiness to read. A person can force-feed reading material to the child when he is only two and by dint of sheer effort help the child to learn to read. For a while he will be ahead of others his age. Because the parents forced their child to learn to read before he was ready, however, thus working against God's timetable, they will suddenly see many of his friends his age catching up with him at about five or six, when all children develop the readiness to read. Some will even pass him. What took the pushy parents hours of concentrated effort to teach their son *before* he was ready, others will learn with amazing speed because they *are* ready.

We similarly develop a readiness to break a bad habit. Don taught me this. I used to joke with him about his weight, but underlying my joking was a real concern for him, and he knew it. Then things began to change between Don and his Lord. God began to do marvelous things in his life. As this was happening, I joked with him one time about losing some weight. But with keen insight into the Spirit's methods, he said, "God's doing too many other things in my life right now for me to lose weight. When He gets ready the pounds will roll off." He was right. About a year later, he felt it was God's time to take off some weight. In the course of six months he lost almost 100 pounds. The Spirit worked; Don accepted his responsiblity; and the time was right. When the time is right, a habit can be easy to break.

Assignment:

1. Seek God's forgiveness for past failures.
2. List other people whom your habit has hurt. Seek their forgiveness.
3. Forgive yourself.
4. Memorize Romans 5:8 and 8:33.

Further reading:

Bill Counts and Bruce Narramore, *Freedom from Guilt* (Zondervan).

Lorne Sanny, *How to Spend a Day in Prayer* (NavPress).

10

Dealing with Anger

Anger. How do you deal with it? Shove it down where it will sneak back to attack you later? Consciously turn it aside for later work? Explode like an antipersonnel bomb, scattering fragments around that hurt anyone who doesn't dive for cover? Or do you quietly make it known, seeking to deal honestly with your anger? I want to suggest you learn to express you anger in a straightforward, nonthreatening way.

Controlling anger is an important part of breaking a bad habit, because fear of or inability to control anger keeps you from effectively controlling habits that grow out of anger. In fact, bad habits are often a way of dealing with anger. This is particularly the case with seemingly compulsive habits like overeating, drinking, procrastination, drug addiction, fingernail biting, knuckle cracking, and many others.

You can't deal effectively with anger unless you begin by admitting you're angry. Simple as that may appear, for many people it is not easy. The Bible tells us, "The heart is the most deceitful thing there is, and desperately wicked. No one can really know how bad it is" (Jer. 17:9). You often may not realize you're angry while you're angry. And afterward, it's not unusual to be unaware you were angry. Thus, acknowledging it when you're angry isn't always easy. You may even need help to recognize it.

Two biblical illustrations demonstrate unrecognized and unacknowledged anger. After Absalom killed his half-brother Amnon because Amnon raped Absalom's sister, their father, David, was angry with Absalom. He recognized it to begin with, but he did nothing about it. Eventually Absalom asked David's forgiveness and apparently received it, but David never gave up his anger. He allowed Absalom to return to Jerusalem, but he refused to see him. Eventually David's unacknowledged anger led to his son's death.

Jonah was also an angry man — but at God. However, he didn't acknowledge his anger until God, through a series of difficult experiences and pointed questions, drew him out to keep him from destroying himself with his anger.

To learn how to recognize when you're angry, you'll probably need to ask for help. In some instances, other people will help you without knowing it. In others, a few friends will help you if you ask them to.

How can people help you without realizing it? First, ask yourself, is the person you're talking to getting angry? This usually indicates that you're angry and the other person is responding in a like manner. Anger sparks anger, as Solomon said: "A soft answer turns away wrath, but harsh words cause quarrels" (Prov. 15:1). The next time you think this might be happening, do two things. Challenge yourself with the question, "Am I angry right now?" Or ask the other person, "Is my behavior or tone of voice making you think I'm angry?" If he says yes, trust his judgement.

Family members are particularly adept at reading your emotions. In fact, a basic principle in family living is that your family members often know your emotional state better than you do. Why? Because they need to learn how to read your emotions to survive living with you. So if a family member comments on your anger, you're probably angry.

I generally assume that when my wife tells me I'm angry, I am, even when I don't sense it. When we were first married, I remember getting very hostile with a parking lot attendant. He saw me come out of the store his parking lot served. But because I had forgotten to get my parking ticket stamped along with my purchase, he was going to charge me for parking, even though the store offered free parking to its customers. I never realized I was angry until my wife pointed it out. Then I saw how I'd failed in dealing with the man.

Sudden silence also communicates anger. If you're talking with a person and he suddenly refuses to respond, you're probably angry. Because most people both fear anger and also realize you can't reason with an angry person, they clam up when someone gets angry. This means that if people around you suddenly get quiet, there's a good chance you're angry.

A recent parenting seminar I conducted illustrates this. After my presentation, I opened the meeting for questions. One woman immediately attacked me for my position on spanking children. When she was finished, I failed to recognize how angry I was, so I attacked right back. I even used the horrible put-down, "When you say that, you're arguing against the Bible." She stopped talking and refused to respond to any further questions from me. It was then that I realized I was angry, but I must admit that even then I failed to confess that to the group as I should have.

Withdrawal also reveals anger. Withdrawal is different from silence in that the person now almost "climbs into a shell," continuing the conversation only through short, terse answers. This again shelters people from dealing with anger, but it also tells you you're angry.

You need more help, though, than simply reading other people's behavior. Some people can tell you directly when you're angry. I've already mentioned family. When they tell you you're angry, you are. You can't really deny it. But close friends can also help if you work out a signal they can give you. When I play baseball, a situation in which I have a tendency to lose control, I ask a friend to speak sharply to me to warn me to calm down.

Through prayer, the Holy Spirit can also help you uncover your anger. Once when David struggled with a problem, he prayed, "Search me, O God, and know my heart; Try me and know my anxious thoughts; And see if there be any hurtful way in me" (Ps. 139:23-24, NASB). David knew the Holy Spirit could uncover sins he didn't know about or was hiding. You, too, need the Spirit's assistance as you seek to deal with your anger.

You can also uncover anger in yourself by learning the special behaviors you engage in when you're angry. For example, when I get angry, the first thing I do is drop my voice to a lower register. I also speak very softly. I carefully consider each word, sometimes speaking with such precision that I actually choke on my words. I note as well that my heart beats more rapidly and I feel flushed, or warm.

What are your angry behaviors? Some people shout; others cry. Some people walk out of the room without a word, while others stomp out, slamming doors and making all sorts of noise. Some people clench their fists, while others get weak in the knees. Some people talk nonstop, while others get so tongue-tied they can't speak (or they stutter or stammer). Some develop facial tics. All sorts of things might happen, but what happens to you?

If you want to gain control of your bad habit, you have to learn to control your anger. You can't do this until you know you're angry. So write out what you do when you get angry. This is important, because many bad habits are a response to unexpressed anger.

You Are What You Think

Remember our talk about A-B-C? It's not what happens that matters (A) so much as what you tell yourself about what happens (B) — that determines your response (C). I assume that no one is responsible for your emotions other than you. No one else can make you angry. You get angry because of what you tell yourself in response to some event in your life. If that's true, then we need to ask concerning your anger, "What are you telling yourself that is making you angry?"

Think back to the last time you knew you were angry. What did you tell yourself that made you angry? Write it out. Now, using our challenge questions, ask "Is that logical?" "Is it a statement others would support?" "Is there an alternative explanation that might be better?" "Is the statement biblical?" By challenging your statement, you may discover you had no reason to be angry. Prayerfully ask the Holy Spirit for wisdom in discovering effective challenges when you get angry. (This, of course, applies only to those situations where your anger is not right — probably most of them.) Unless you develop the ability to challenge your angry statements, you'll have a hard time controlling your anger.

Let's look at Jonah's response again (Jonah 4). He got angry with God for being merciful when Nineveh repented of its sin, because he hated the Ninevites and wanted to see them destroyed. Then he mourned the loss of a vine shading him from the sun as he sat on a hillside, waiting for God to destroy the city. Since Jonah wouldn't challenge the validity of his own self-talk, God did it for him, showing him how foolish it was to be angry about the death of a vine while still wishing for the death of hundreds of thousands of people.

Interpersonal relationships with family members probably generate more anger than anything else life offers. Early in my married life, I often blamed my wife for not meeting various needs I had. I became quite angry, sometimes stewing for several days about what happened. Then I began to challenge my self-talk. *Is she deliberately trying to hurt me?* I had to admit she probably wasn't. *Is my response of brooding anger biblical?* Far from it. *Is my response logical?* Not really. I should have been talking with her rather than brooding in anger. Slowly these challenges pulled the stinger from my anger and helped us work out a more satisfying relationship. But it could not happen until I carefully analyzed the self-talk that made me angry, and then challenged it.

Having determined now what you said to yourself that made you angry, you have an obligation to challenge those statements. Only by showing, under the Holy Spirit's direction, that other statements are equally satisfying can you change your emotional response away from anger. The less anger you have in your life, the more control you will have over your habits.

Slow Down

James told us to slow down if we want to control our anger: "Dear brothers, don't ever forget that it is best to listen much, speak little, and not become angry; for anger doesn't make us good, as God demands that we must be" (1:19-20). Popular wisdom says the same thing. "Count to ten before you get angry." Why? Because it gives you time to think before you say or do something you may later regret.

What should you think about? I like to think by asking questions that help me understand the other person's position. I try to ask questions that help me get at motives and goals behind people's actions. Why? Because I've discovered that most of the time when I get angry at other people it's because I don't understand what they are doing or saying. If I can ask enough polite questions, I can often learn about their actions so that I reduce or even eliminate my anger. Many times, simply understanding another person's motives will break my balloon of anger.

My wife and I recently learned this when our pharmacy and doctor got their signals crossed. Our youngest son, Peter, ran a high fever for a couple of days, so we called the doctor to see if he wanted to see him or just write a prescription. The receptionist told us the doctor would get back with us later, but he didn't. Four days later, our middle son, Jon needed medication following surgery, so we went to the pharmacy to get it. When we got there, they informed us that Peter's prescription had been waiting for us for four days.

It would have been easy for me to blow up in anger when I heard that. But when we went to the doctor's office and asked why they never called back, they explained that it was an oversight. They knew we were upset, and they apologized. And then we established a plan to keep the problem from being repeated in the future.

Another simple device that gives you time to think is to take five deep breaths before you speak when you feel yourself getting angry.

What you need to do now is write out a plan to control your anger when you feel it developing. Ask the Holy Spirit to guide you as you write out what you are going to do to slow your angry reactions next time you sense them coming. Then use the plan you create.

Communicate Your Anger

Next, communicate your anger in a way that does not threaten others. Ephesians 4:25 says, "Stop lying to each other; tell the truth, for we are parts of each other and when we lie to each other we are hurting ourselves." To pretend you're not angry when you are is to lie. Most people think it's hurtful to express your anger to others. But it's not hurtful to express your anger if you plan a low-threat message that focuses on your reaction rather than the other person's fault. But make sure you communicate that *you* are angry. Never blame another person for causing your anger. Remember that you get angry as a result of what you tell yourself about what happened, not as a direct consequence of the event itself.

You might handle the situation like this: "I feel angry right now. I'm responding to what you just said [did], but I need your help to deal with my anger. Would you help me?" This does a number of good things. First, it lets the person know you're angry — he probably already knew, but now it's out in the open. Second, it puts him in the position of helping you, something we all like to do. Third, it involves him in the solution to your anger, and this is good because you're reacting to him. Revealing your feelings in this manner doesn't start fights or hurt people, as most people imagine. Instead, it usually leads to a good discussion that deals with the source of your anger and reduces or eliminates it.

I saw this in a conversation with the police about child abuse. One of my boy's friends came to visit sporting a huge black eye and a number of large bruises. I jokingly asked what happened and she responded, "Oh, that's where Daddy hit me." Since her response startled me, I asked a few more questions and learned he beat her regularly.

Later that day I visited the sheriff's office and expressed my concern for the little girl. The officer in charge said, "Oh, that's a matter for Social Services, we don't investigate child abuse."

I immediately experienced a surge of anger. I said, "I respond to your statement with anger. It seems to me that you are ducking your responsibility."

She replied, "Not really. We don't have the skills to investigate child abuse, while the Department of Social Services does. If they discover anything wrong, they tell us and we follow up on it." She accepted my anger and dealt with my problem without taking offense.

Overcome Your Anger

Finally, develop ways to overcome your anger. One tool I've learned to use is a promise not to attack the person but to focus on the problem. I tell the person as I start the conversation that I'm angry and want to solve a problem. I then promise not to attack him but to stay with the problem. (This is a very effective tool when marriage partners fight.)

I first tried this in the special meeting I had with the church board a couple of months after I lost my position there. Even before we began our discussion, I told them, "Fellows, I'm still very angry about what happened, and I'm not sure I can completely control my anger during this meeting. I promise, though, that I won't attack any of you personally. I also want to arrange a time-out signal with you before we start. I'm doing this so we can resolve our differences, not intensify our anger." What followed was a tense but productive meeting.

A promise not to attack is not enough. Understanding comes next. Seek to discover what the other person was trying to say or do at the time you got angry. Explain what you were trying to say or do yourself. Ask yourself what might have happened earlier that contributed to your feelings at the time (a bad day, an earlier fight, a headache, etc.). Asking questions and listening are excellent ways to overcome anger, because they promote understanding. This also helps you discover the real cause of your anger so you can actually deal with it rather than with a side issue. (As this conversation is going on, silently ask the Holy Spirit for help in controlling your anger.)

Sometimes the other person isn't around when you get angry. What then? Carefully think out a positive conversation with him. Again, ask the Holy Spirit to guide you to speak wisely and as calmly as possible. Then be firm and open, but not aggressive. If you carefully think out what you plan to say, you bring your emotions more under control and can focus on solving the problem rather than hurting the other person or just getting your own way.

As with all married couples, my wife, Geri, and I occasionally have difficulties. Before I talk with her about what is bothering me, I try to think through carefully just what I want to say. This may take time, but I've learned that if I don't take time before speaking, I'll probably have to take it afterward to clear up misunderstandings. I need to speak very carefully when I'm angry, and so do you.

A word of caution: Not everyone is interested in a good relationship with you. When you reveal your anger, some people will care little or nothing about how you feel. There are such people, and there's not much you can do about them. But with most people, the method outlined here works.

Finally, if you want to deal successfully with anger, you need to learn to view life from God's perspective. This means that you recognize the trials of life as one of God's primary tools in developing Christian maturity. James 1:2-4 says,

> Dear brothers, is your life full of difficulties and temptations? Then be happy, for when the way is rough, your patience has a chance to grow. So let it grow, and don't try to squirm out of your problems. For when your patience is finally in full bloom, then you will be ready for anything, strong in character, full and complete.

It also means you will expect to be treated as Jesus was. Though He lived a perfect life, He was still persecuted. He warned His disciples in John 15:20, "Do you remember what I told you? 'A slave isn't greater than his master!' So since they persecuted Me, naturally they will persecute you. And if they had listened to Me, they would listen to you!" Expect the same mistreatment as Jesus received, and it will diminish your anger.

Next, in dealing with anger, recognize that nothing can sever your relationship with God. All the losses and crosses of life will never compare with eternity spent with God. Paul put it this way in Romans 8:18: "Yet what we suffer now is nothing compared to the glory He will give us later." Develop Paul's attitude and your problems with anger will quickly recede.

You also need to realize that God is sufficient to create good out of the worst experiences you have. I like to paraphrase Romans 8:28 as saying, "In the midst of my experiences of life, God is at work for good because I love Him and have been called according to His purpose." This tells me I will encounter all sorts of evil as I walk this earth, but it also gives me the assurance that even in the midst of that evil, God is at work to create something valuable for me.

Finally, life viewed from God's perspective recognizes that

you've been called to minister to others in Jesus' name. No situation arises in which you cannot minister if you will creatively seek the Spirit's guidance to see the opportunities for ministry around you. This attitude also helps you control your anger by focusing on others' needs above your own.

But I have to admit that I don't always control my anger. What happens when you fail to deal with anger in a Christian manner? You either attack the other person, pout for days, or simply walk away and brood about what happened, carrying on your own guerrilla warfare against the person with whom you're angry.

In other words, your anger becomes sin.

When that happens, you go to the instructions on seeking forgiveness in the previous chapter. Unresolved guilt about your anger can be a key element in destroying your plan to deal with your bad habit.

Assignment:

1. Write a description of your angry behavior, both what happens inside and what happens outside.
2. Write out what you told yourself that made you angry in a recent incident in your life.
3. Write out a personal plan to slow your anger reactions.

Further reading:

Charles Cerling, *Assertiveness and the Christian* (Tyndale).
H. Norman Wright, *Dealing with Frustration and Anger* (Harvest House).

11

Dealing with Anxiety

Tension and anxiety are probably two of the biggest reasons people continue habits they know are hurting them. Yet many people run from the problems that cause their anxiety. This may seem short-sighted, but most people would rather avoid anxiety and postpone dealing with the problems than experience a little anxiety now while finding a solution to the problems.

Let's assume for a moment that you have a problem at work. As you and your fellow workers have talked, you've discovered that you're being underpaid. The other people who do the same work as you receive more, even though you've been on the job at least as long as they have. You're upset, but you hate the thought of having to face your boss about this unfairness. In fact, you can actually feel your stomach tighten as you think about talking to him. Your mind races with all the things that might go wrong. You might be fired; you might be demoted; he might cancel your vacation; and on and on and on. The more you think about talking to him, the more anxious you become.

Because you dislike the feelings of anxiety you experience when you think about talking to your boss, you decide to say nothing. However, this means you will continue to feel cheated, and that will produce a different kind of tension. What you've done is solve the short-term problem — your anxiety — but you've left the long-term problem — your feeling that you've been cheated. You simply can't solve the long-term problem, though, unless you're willing to face your anxiety.

Worry and Anxiety

Worry. Anxiety. You probably think of them as being just about identical. While I've used them as synonyms so far, I don't really think of them as the same thing. Anxiety is a feeling of tension, uneasiness, apprehension — a general feeling of negative expectations. Worry, on the other hand, usually relates to something specific. I can write out precisely what it is that I'm worrying about.

Let's consider our illustration of talking with the boss about a raise. That's really more worry than anxiety. The boss might do any one of the things you thought about. There's reason for worry.

But let's imagine that the boss is the most easygoing fellow you've ever met. You've never seen him get really angry. Whenever you've asked for a raise in the past, he's given it to you. Once he didn't, but then the company had just come through hard times, and he carefully explained why he couldn't give you a raise before he said no. He's even let you take a day off whenever you've wanted it. Does that mean you'll be perfectly calm and relaxed when you talk to him? Not on your life! Any time you talk with someone about something that is important to you, particularly when you feel misused, you experience anxiety. Many people describe this by saying they have a problem with their nerves.

So we see that while worry is different from anxiety, they can't be entirely separated. But in this chapter I want to deal exclusively with the feelings of tension you experience that don't have an obvious cause. I want to do this because many bad habits are ways of dealing with this tension.

Let me begin with this caution: Such tension is not always bad. As a minister, I do a good deal of public speaking. Whenever I speak in public, no matter how well prepared I am, I'm tense and anxious. I've spoken with other ministers about this and discovered that I'm not alone. They all experience tension or anxiety each time they stand up in front of a group. Are they afraid of failing? Not really. They simply want to do a good job, and therefore they experience a mild tension that actually helps them perform.

What this means is that the right amount of anxiety is actually good for you. When you are perfectly calm in a situation that demands a mild level of tension, you can't perform well. As I mentioned earlier, I manage a Little League team during the summers. Each time a pitch is thrown, some boys get right up on their toes, ready to go wherever the ball is hit. Others stand flat-footed, relaxed, as they watch the action. Guess who plays better? Certainly, the boys who are mildly tense in anticipation of the action. I'm not so much concerned about anxiety itself as I am about anxiety that keeps you from doing a good job and therefore also often contributes to a bad habit. You want to overcome this type of anxiety.

Dealing with Anxiety

If anxiety is not all bad, you have to make a judgement about the situations you face. Namely, what level of anxiety is appropriate in each case? When my oldest boy, David, began playing the piano in public, he was so concerned he might make a mistake that he couldn't play well. That's too much anxiety, but it's probably to be expected when you begin something public and new. On the other hand, let's imagine you are sitting in your back yard basking in the summer sun, yet you feel highly anxious. In this case, this level of anxiety is not proper. All of this illustrates that anxiety must be appropriate to the situation. Put another way, each situation demands a different level of anxiety.

As a means of helping you determine what level of anxiety is appropriate to a particular situation, psychologists have developed what they call the SUDS scale (Subjective Units of Disturbance Scale). It's a scale that represents your anxiety level in a range between 0 and 100, and it's totally subjective.

You determine the zero end of the scale by picturing yourself in the most relaxing situation you can imagine. You determine the 100 end of the scale by projecting yourself into the most anxiety-provoking situation you can envision. Everything else falls somewhere in between.

For example, imagine how you would feel if you were asked to speak in church next week before the whole congregation. Where would you place your expected level of anxiety? 25? 50? 75? 90? Or let's say the school called and told you they caught your son smoking marijuana. Where would your anxiety level be when you talked with the authorities? 15? 40? 65? No matter what you're dealing with, you can rank it on the SUDS scale. But only you can do it, since this is a purely subjective measurement. In addition, you're the only one who can determine where you want your SUDS score to be for any given event. While I'm speaking, a SUDS score of 25 might be normal. But if you're not accustomed to speaking, a score of 50 might be anticipated. Neither is wrong.

You can determine your anxiety level also by your eye contact. In normal conversation, people regularly look into the other person's eyes, glance away for a moment, then look them in the eye again. When you begin to look more at the floor, ceiling, your feet, hands, or anywhere else, your anxiety level is pretty high.

Posture, another indicator of anxiety, is measured by extremes rather than by graduated steps. You're either all right, too rigid, or too relaxed. It's impossible to play an athletic game well and be perfectly relaxed. On the other hand, some people get so tense when they appear in public that they limit their ability to perform. Posture is either appropriate or inappropriate, with a very wide range covering normal.

Nervous laughter and joking also reveal your anxiety level. Joyce decided to be a missionary when she was in her early fifties. She revealed her chosen field and missionary plans in an evening service on Sunday. As she spoke, she told silly jokes and made offhand remarks totally inappropriate to the situation and far removed from her normal character. Then she giggled in a high-pitched laugh that was quite distracting. Phyllis watched in astonishment. *Joyce is making a fool of herself*, she thought. She couldn't believe her ears or eyes. But Joyce was simply showing everyone how nervous she was while speaking in church.

Excessive or unrelated head, hand, or body movements further reveal anxiety. As a counselor, I watch people's hands and feet during counseling, because they often tell me when the person is getting upset. Occasionally I see a public speaker who looks like a windmill because of his hand motions, but he's simply letting me know he's nervous.

If you combine these four physical indicators with your SUDS scale, you have a fair indication of your anxiety level.

Then you have to ask yourself, "Is this appropriate? Is it too much? Is it too little?" Only you can determine what is appropriate for you in any given situation. But once you've determined what is appropriate, you can decide what you want to do about it so it doesn't contribute to your bad habit.

Part of dealing with anxiety comes from learning about God's role as our loving heavenly Father. As a father, I know the amount of time and effort I spend seeking to meet the needs in my children's lives. God as my heavenly Father has so much more wisdom and power than I will ever have that His concern for me must be far beyond anything I feel for my children. This means, then, that I need to rest secure in His love. As I learn to do this, my anxiety level in general will come down, because all anxiety is at least in part a result of insecurity.

Finally, you might not be able to deal with your anxiety by yourself. In this short chapter, I've suggested various means that work for many people. I'll suggest a few more. But anxiety can be a very serious problem. If it's a long-term problem in your life, talk with your pastor or a professional counselor. Either should be able to help you work through problems related to anxiety.

Learn to Relax

"If you just relax, you won't have any problems." How many times have you heard that advice? Though it may be true, it's very difficult for most people to do, because they've never learned how to relax. While I want to use the remainder of this chapter to develop a psychological tool to help you relax, we also need to examine briefly some common-sense helps in relaxing.

1. *Don't schedule more in a given day than you can handle.* Most people keep themselves running through life, when God would rather you'd walk and enjoy the world He put you in. Part of the running is the result of poor time management, an area in which we can all improve. But part of it is simply scheduling more things than you can reasonably handle. (For more on this, see *The Tyranny of the Urgent*, a booklet from NavPress.)

2. *Another means of tension reduction is getting regular*

exercise. One of God's more important means of relieving our bodies of stress is regular exercise. Many bad habits simply slip away when you exercise regularly, because exercise reduces the tension you're used to reducing through your bad habit. I particularly feel this living in northern Michigan in the winter time. I frequently have to deal with tension during our long winters, when I can become rather anxious. But I've found that if I can get out and exercise regularly, the tensions diminish.

3. *The other side of regular exercise is adequate rest.* You cannot effectively fight temptation when you are constantly tired. And lack of sleep contributes to tension in your life. Thus, sleeping regular hours and getting a full night's rest will help reduce your tension.

4. *You also need to eat right.* Increasingly, doctors are discovering that simply eating right, particularly reducing your intake of sugar, caffeine, and salt, is a means of reducing tension.

5. *Develop something you can do just for fun.* We Christians are often so caught up with the seriousness of life that we don't leave enough time for fun. But few things reduce tension more effectively than a plain, old-fashioned good time. (For more information, see *When I Relax I Feel Guilty,* by Tim Hansel and published by David C. Cook.)

6. *For the Christian, a key means of reducing tension is maintaining a regular devotional life.* When you are regularly letting God talk with you through His Word and then responding to Him in prayer, you will reduce the level of tension in your life. As you respond to God, you develop His perspective on the problems of your life, and they seem smaller, thus reducing your tension.

Now let's look at the psychological tool, which involves deep muscle relaxation. I want you to practice this in private so that you can eventually transfer it over into public when you find yourself becoming tense and anxious. To do this, tense the muscles in one of the groups listed below for about five to seven seconds. Then relax completely for about twenty to thirty seconds. Do this for each muscle group in turn.

After a while, you'll find yourself relaxing without any difficulty. Then you can transfer the exercise to everyday life.

When you sense tenseness in a particular muscle group, you'll be able to focus your mind on that group and consciously relax it. This does wonders in reducing tension and, with it, anxiety. I have used this method for years in the pulpit. When I discover I'm getting tense, I grip the shelf of a pulpit with my hand until I almost cramp. This focuses all my tension into my arm, removing it from my face and throat, where it hinders my speaking. Then I let go and find I've relaxed all over.

Below is the order of major muscle groups to be relaxed.

1. Tense the muscles in your right hand by making a fist.
2. Tense the muscles in your right upper arm. Bend your arm at the elbow, and make a muscle.
3. Tense the muscles in your left hand by making a fist.
4. Tense the muscles in your left upper arm. Bend your arm at the elbow, and make a muscle.
5. Tense the muscles in your forehead by frowning.
6. Tense the muscles in your eyes by closing your eyes tightly.
7. Tense the muscles in your nose by wrinkling it.
8. Tense the muscles in your lips and lower face by pressing your lips together tightly and forcing your tongue against the top of your mouth.
9. Tense the muscles in your jaw by clenching your teeth together.
10. Tense the muscles in your neck by attempting to look directly above you.
11. Tense the muscles in your shoulders and upper back by shrugging your shoulders.
12. Tense the muscles in your chest by taking a deep breath and holding it.
13. Tense the muscles in the small of your back by arching up your back.
14. Tense the muscles in your abdomen by either pushing those muscles out or pulling them in.
15. Tense the muscles in your buttocks and thighs by pressing your heels into the floor.
16. Tense the muscles in your ankles and calves by pointing them away from your body.

Practice these exercises daily, and you will notice that they will increase your ability to relax in tense situations.

Assignment:

1. Examine your life based on the six common-sense tension reducers, and make needed changes.
2. Memorize and meditate on Romans 8:38,39.
3. Practice deep muscle relaxation.

Further Reading:

H. Norman Wright, *Dealing with Worry and Anxiety* (Harvest House).

12

Competing Replacement Behavior

For a moment, let's imagine that your bad habit is finger-nail biting. You come to me with your problem and ask me how you can break it. I immediately respond, "Buy a pair of surgeon's gloves and wear them all the time, since you can't bite your fingernails while you have gloves on. If you feel you might bite you nails even through the gloves (some people would), spend each day sitting on your hands, since you can't bite what you can't reach." You would probably get up and walk out. You would also tell your friends about the nut you ran into who claimed to be a counselor.

Yet my illustration shows an element of breaking a habit that people often miss. You can't *not* think or *not* do something. If you're going to break a bad habit, you have to develop some form of competing replacement behavior. However, as our illustration showed, there are many different varieties of replacement behavior. The ones I suggested above obviously would work, but they are just as obviously totally impractical. So let's see what kinds of replacement behavior will help you.

Characteristics of Competing Replacement Behavior

1. It is incompatible with your present habit.
2. It does not attract the attention of other people
3. It does not interfere with normal living.
4. It does draw your attention to your bad habit.

First, *replacement behavior should be incompatible with your habit.* That is, when you are engaging in your replacement behavior, it should be impossible to engage in your habit. Wearing gloves as a means of stopping fingernail biting fits that qualification, but it's impractical. A better example would be my friend who quit smoking by keeping a cigarette holder in his pocket. Each time he felt the urge to smoke, he pulled the cigarette holder out and put it in his mouth. But many people would feel ridiculous doing that. Thus, a smoker might choose to put a toothpick in his mouth each time he feels the need to light up. Even less conspicuously, he might want to pop a piece of gum into his mouth, since the saliva generated by gum tends to make smoking unpleasant. Whatever you choose, however, it should be something that quite literally keeps you from engaging in the habit you want to break. That's not always easy, but it is necessary. Ask the Holy Spirit for help in discovering a behavior that works for your habit.

When Diane came to me and described her problem with a critical spirit, I was stumped. I had struggled with this problem for a long time in my own life, and at first I thought she would just have to live with it. But her question got me to thinking. What can a person do that will actively compete with a critical spirit? The more I thought about it, the more excited I became. A person who regularly criticizes or thinks critically about others can use two substitute behaviors. For one thing, critical thinking can be used as a springboard to prayer. When I see something I want to criticize, I pray about it. On the other hand, I can immediately force myself to think about things in the person's life that I would like to praise. I can then use my critical spirit as a means of forcing my mind into channels of praise.

The second qualification is the one that eliminates gloves or sitting on your hands. *Competing behavior should not draw the attention of other people to itself.* It should be something you can do naturally. If you feel conspicuous while using your replacement behavior, you will hesitate often enough that you will have a hard time breaking your habit. Gum chewing is sufficiently common that no one would notice it.

As an example, let's see if we can't develop a behavior that will solve the problem of speaking out too quickly and without thought. The competing replacement behavior would be to ask a question before you make a statement. Thus, when Jesus told the disciples they would all abandon Him when He was arrested, Peter would not have jumped in with his declaration of loyalty. Instead he would have responded, "Lord when I've been so faithful in the past, why will I abandon you now?" While the same fervor might affect the question, it would keep Peter from making a fool of himself with declarations he could not keep.

Third, *competing replacement behavior should not interfere with your normal activities.* Can you imagine attempting to carry out your daily chores while wearing gloves? Impossible! Thus, you have to select something you can do that will permit you to perform the duties of a normal day. The competing replacement behavior for fingernail biting is clenching your hands into a fist or grasping an object near you at the moment of temptation. You do this for only three minutes. In either instance, you can continue the chores you are doing while at the same time preventing yourself from biting your nails.

Let's look at the very common habit of worrying. What can a person do for competing replacement behavior? One of the most effective tools in dealing with worry is the creation of a "to-do" list. When you begin to worry about something, you immediately write it down and a time when you can deal with it. Writing it down takes it from your mind, because you plan on dealing with it later. Writing it down also often reveals that there is nothing you can do about it, such as when you're worrying about the weather. Thus, the to-do list competes with your worrying by destroying the basis for worrying.

Finally, *your replacement behavior should draw your own attention to your habit.* Clenching your hands into a fist requires you to concentrate on what you're doing; thus, it draws attention to your fingernail-biting habit. Your replacement behavior then continues the process started earlier of sensitizing yourself to your habit. This in turn helps you become aware of when you are doing it.

Let's look at a more complicated habit, driving too fast. A good replacement behavior is concentrating on driving five miles per hour below the speed limit. Out of courtesy for others, this means that when cars begin to line up behind you, you periodically pull off the road for a moment to let them pass. Driving below the speed limit also focuses your attention on your problem. Finally, it certainly makes it impossible to drive above the limit, since you can't be below and above at the same time.

If your replacement behavior is going to work, however, you also need to become aware of the preliminary indications of your habit. Such preliminary signals tell you that you are actually beginning to engage in your habit, and you need to start your replacement behavior. As I've said, a habit is not an isolated event. It is usually a prominent event in a series of smaller events. If you can start to deal with it earlier in the series by becoming aware of preliminary behaviors, you can head off the habit before you actually engage in it.

Fingernail biters, for example, touch their heads and faces far more frequently than other people. They touch their faces, their noses, their ears, around their eyes, and their lips far more often than non-biters. They also touch their fingers more frequently than other people. They run their fingers over their other fingers, looking for rough spots. They pick at loose skin or rough edges. They run rough spots on their nails over their other fingers. These are all preliminary actions that eventually lead them to move their fingers into their mouths for biting. Each of these actions needs to become a signal to engage in competing replacement behavior — immediately — before fingernail biting can take place.

What preliminary behaviors signal the onset of your habit? Ask the Holy Spirit to help you discover them. In addition, part of developing a competing replacement behavior that will work for you is returning to your earlier habit analysis. What need did you discover was being met by your habit? Your competing replacement behavior should be a more socially approved or nonsinful way of meeting that need.

All of this takes us back to the story of the Indian medicine man who sold the powder that turned into gold when mixed with water. He knew people could not *not* think about the little red monkeys. You also cannot *not* practice your bad habit unless you first find an acceptable competing replacement behavior. This may take time, but it is too important to lay aside and think you can do everything else without it. Don't attempt to break your bad habit until you have worked out what you think is a good starting replacement behavior.

Practice

When you have developed your own replacement behavior, tailored specifically to your habit and your needs, practice it until you are comfortable with it. The best way to practice is in front of a mirror. This also will help you develop a replacement behavior that can be carried out with the least amount of show. You don't want your behavior to be so conspicuous that you are embarrassed to do it.

Then, as you become comfortable with your behavior, practice working through a situation in which you would normally have trouble. Imagine just what you would do in a step-by-step walk-through of the events. Do this fifteen minutes each day for a week before actually attempting to break your habit. Then continue it five minutes daily for the next three weeks, or until you feel confident you have broken your habit.

As you gain confidence in winning over your bad habit, take on situations that used to be hard for you. Go right in the lion's den, grab your bad habit by his chin hair, and pull him out. You cannot say you have broken your habit until you feel you can go anywhere and still come out all right. But don't start with the toughest situations. Begin with easier situations and work up toward the harder ones. Eventually you should be able to go wherever you used to have the greatest trouble and come away victorious. (On the other hand, if any relapse into your habit could have especially bad consequences — as is the case with alcoholics, for example — you might be better advised to avoid extremely tempting situations as much as possible, even after your habit is under control.)

If you had trouble with overeating, eventually you should be able to go to a fine restaurant with no fear that you will eat too much — even when someone else is paying the bill. If you were a smoker, you can even sit in the dentist's office waiting for an appointment that is an hour late and never touch a cigarette. You will challenge your most troublesome opponent and win. (Remember, however, my earlier admonition to seek professional counsel for serious problem habits, especially those that involve chemical — physical — as well as emotional dependency.)

Rewards

Breaking a bad habit is not enough incentive in itself for many people. The long-term goal appears to be so far away that the immediate pleasure of the bad habit seems too much. For this reason, you should build into your plan for change both minor rewards for success and minor punishments for failure. The minor punishment I suggest for most people is simple. Put a rubber band around your wrist. Each time you fail, pull the rubber band up from your arm a few inches and let it snap down. The punishment is mild and will cause no permanent damage, but the pain is just enough to encourage you to succeed.

Rewards are more individualized. You need to plan something small, just as the punishment for failure is small. We don't want you to feel guilty about rewarding yourself. But the reward should also be something immediate. If you have to wait too long for the reward, it will lose its effectiveness. For some people, simply keeping a diary where they can write down that they won a battle over temptation is enough. Some might want to keep a pocket (purse) full of small change (nickels or dimes). Each victory is then rewarded by payment of one coin. The coins accumulate for some larger reward in the future. The underlying idea remains, however, to do something for yourself that will say, "You did it! Great!"

Measures of Change

1. Shorter periods of temptation.
2. Decreased intensity of temptation.
3. Fewer and fewer failures, with longer and longer periods of victory.

Change, however, is an elusive factor for many people, because they don't really know what they mean by change. When I'm helping a person break a bad habit, I focus on three different measures of change. I want the person's temptations or lapses to diminish in duration, to decrease in intensity, and to diminish in frequency.

When Mike began working on breaking his smoking habit,

we set up a chart to record the temptations he experienced and to measure these change elements. Whenever he was tempted to smoke, he would note how many minutes the temptation lasted. As he grew in his ability to resist temptation, he noted that the temptations didn't last as long as they had when he started. He also noted that his temptations were not so intense. When he began, we devised a scale of intensity going from one to ten. Mike rated the intensity of his temptation by writing down whether the temptation was relatively mild (2) or more intense (8). As time went by, he saw that his temptations also diminished by an intensity (7, 5, 4). He also noted the frequency of his temptations. When he began, he felt the urge to smoke as often as 20 times daily. As time went on, the urge came less frequently.

Any indication of change is a measure of success. Whether the duration of the temptation is less, the intensity has diminished, or the temptations come less frequently, you are succeeding. Each measure of change reveals a move in the direction of victory.

Change Chart

Date	Duration (mins.)	Intensity (1-10)	Frequency
2 - 9	8, 3, 10, 7, 9, 5, 8, 9, 7,	10, 5, 10, 9, 8, 7, 9, 10,	⊞ℍ IIII
2 - 10	9, 7, 8, 10, 7, 4, 6, 8, 5,	10, 6, 8, 7, 9, 5, 7,	⊞ℍ III
2 - 11	8, 7, 8, 6, 9, 3, 5, 7, 4,	8, 7, 9, 6, 7, 5, 4,	⊞ℍ III

Change Chart

Date	Duration (mins.)	Intensity (1-10)	Frequency

Use daily until you are satisfied.
Keep notes on 3x5 cards when chart isn't available.

Use daily until you are satisfied. Keep notes on 3" x 5" cards when chart isn't available.

Keep in mind that change is rarely constant. Change, if graphed, would be a series of ups and downs, with progress in the direction of success. Almost no one decides to change and from that day forward has fewer and fewer problems. To get to the mountain top, you have to walk through the valleys as well as climb the hills in between.

If you want to change, you need to keep progress records as a means of identifying your changes. These help you measure the changes in duration, intensity, and frequency mentioned earlier.

Progress records also help focus your attention on your successes rather than on your failures. When you get together with a group of people trying to break a bad habit, such as smoking or overeating, listen to their conversation. Do they brag about their successes in resisting temptation? Rarely. They generally focus on the times they failed. But by concentrating on their failures, they are setting themselves up for more failures. A progress record helps you focus on your successes. Particularly on days when you have failed and are discouraged, a progress record helps you see how well you succeeded in the past. It gives perspective in the face of the occasional inevitable failure.

A progress record is also a reward in itself. Every time you look at your achievements, you gain a sense of accomplishment at what you have done.

Persistence

At this point, however, a warning is in order. Don't begin a plan to break a bad habit unless you intend to stick with it until you have changed for good. As noted earlier, a key element in successful efforts to change is motivation. Persistence is as important as any special technique someone might devise. Habits learned over a lifetime usually do not go away overnight. Winning over them often takes time and persistent effort. Unless you have sufficient commitment to stick with it, you shouldn't even begin. Pray regularly that the Holy Spirit will give you persistence and encouragement to continue.

There is a parallel to breaking a bad habit in going to a physician for a prescription. Most doctors' biggest complaint about people taking medicine is that as soon as the obvious symptoms are gone, people quit taking their medicine. Doctors, however, know that obvious symptoms go away long before the disease is actually cured. When a person quits taking the medication as soon as the symptoms disappear, he gives the disease a new opportunity to grow and get worse. Similarly, unless you keep working at habit breaking even when you think you're victorious, you'll probably fall back into your old ways.

Another reason for this warning is that habit change focuses on long-term goals, while American society is oriented toward meeting short-term goals. We focus on gratifying whatever need we have at the moment. Habit change means you have to exchange short-term gratification for the benefits that come from long-term effort. Again, ask the Holy Spirit to help you focus on your long-term goals in the face of short-term difficulties and disappointments.

In addition, changing any major habit generally means reorganizing part of your life. As Marie began working on her weight goal, she slowly realized that eating too much was a much bigger problem than she had imagined. She discovered that she planned food any time a friend came over. She also noted that her family gatherings placed a strong emphasis on food. In her church, many of her friends went out for something to eat each time a meeting concluded. As she watched TV, she nibbled on something. To reach her weight goal, she slowly began to change her living habits, because they contributed to her problem.

You cannot reorganize your lifestyle in a week or two. Such changes take time. You can only do this if you have determined that you are willing to stick with it until you succeed.

Now I want to go through this whole procedure using an elementary habit, nail biting, an old bad habit of mine, as an illustration.

I first discovered the associated habits of touching my face and playing with my fingers. I often read or work with a hand resting on my face. I will play with my fingers around my lips. I also tend to pick at my nails when I'm nervous. Thus, I use these as sensitizing items to tell me I'm moving toward biting my nails.

The replacement behavior is clenching my hand into a fist or grasping something close to me so that my fingers cannot get into my mouth. But since fingernail biting is also a means of tension release, I developed other means of reducing tension in my life. Much of this relates to getting enough exercise and getting out with people so that I'm not bored with what I'm doing. Whenever I feel the urge to bite my nails, I practice my replacement behavior for at least three minutes. This is usually long enough for the urge to go away.

The specific situations in which I have trouble are TV watching, reading my Bible during devotions, and driving the car. Whenever I note myself engaging in behavior that is lead-ing toward biting my nails, I use the replacement behavior. When watching TV, I grasp the chair arms just tight enough that I'm aware of what I'm doing. This both stops me and sensitizes me to what I was about to do. If I'm reading my Bible, I grasp the two sides with both hands. This again sensitizes me while keeping me from biting. If I'm driving the car, I grab the wheel with both hands, since I can't bite my nails when both hands are on the wheel. This is my specific application.

I also noticed when I failed, however, that if I began biting a nail and it had a rough edge, I was particularly prone to go back to that nail and bite it again — to straighten out the rough edge I created earlier. What I needed was something to smooth my nail so I would not have something so obviously tempting. Failure taught me to carry a nail file to smooth all rough edges created by my nail biting. Thus, my failure showed me a particularly difficult temptation with which I had to deal.

Key to all of this is regular practice with competing be-havior. Each day for the first week of attempting to break the habit, I practiced fifteen minutes. After this, for three weeks I practiced five minutes daily. If I had not broken the habit, I would have continued my practice.

We also need to deal with relapses into the old habit. (The concluding chapter spells this out in more detail.) If the habit reappears, you have to begin again with your practice from square one. A habit is not broken when you have a day of freedom. It is broken when you can look back on a month of freedom, a year of freedom. Even then it might recur, but it will be much easier to break.

Periodically, I still have problems with nail biting. But now I look at what is happening in my life. I eliminate all the tensions I can. I also immediately institute the habit-breaking patterns I learned earlier. Within a few days the problem disappears.

As I broke the habit, I began to challenge bad situations. The worst was (and still is) driving. But as I saw what was happening, I changed my driving habits as well as using the habit-breaking technique. I no longer drive as though I'm in a race, and that reduced the tension to the level where fingernail biting is rarely a problem any more.

Now it's your turn. Write out a replacement behavior for your habit. Make sure it meets the qualifications spelled out at the beginning of the chapter. Then make use of it while you're completing this book.

Assignment:

1. Develop and practice a competing replacement behavior for your habit.
2. Plan small rewards for overcoming temptation.
3. Chart the indicators of change as you work on your habit.

Further reading:

Nathan Azrin and R. Gregory Nunn, *Habit Control in a Day* (Pocket Books), ch. 12.

(These men popularized the habit control principles presented in this book, even though they are widely used in the field of psychology.)

13

Family and Friends

Franz came to me off and on for several years for help with a drinking problem. During this past summer he said he had suddenly realized what a serious problem his drinking was. He had gone to the home of two close friends, relating his concern to them. "It suddenly hit me as I was driving home from the Roadhouse Bar that my drinking and the six-pack on the seat beside me were destroying my life." He prayed with those friends, recommitting his life to the Lord.

For the remainder of the summer and into the fall, things went well. Then duck-hunting season began. Franz and his family are avid duck hunters. This is the big event in their family each fall. Each weekend Franz joined them, both because he enjoyed the hunting and because he didn't want to refuse to participate. But in Franz's family, duck hunting included staying warm with a liberal dose of antifreeze in the form of beer. By the end of duck season, Franz was again having drinking problems. The pressure of his family was just too much.

Family and friends can be great sources of support when you are trying to break a bad habit. On the other hand, many studies of the problems surrounding relapse have shown that family and friends are also the greatest single source of temptation. We need to look at both sides of this issue, support and problems.

Support

Let's begin by looking at the support family and friends can give. A major problem in breaking a bad habit is the tendency to try to hide your problem. As a result, you may think others don't know you have a problem; you may be deceiving yourself about how effectively you are hiding it. Actually, however, it's out of politeness and misguided concern that others say nothing unless someone else brings up the subject. But most want to help if only you will be honest about your problem. And as noted in the section on temptation, a feeling of isolation in temptation hurts you. When you admit your need, the feeling of isolation is broken. Maybe this is why James said "Admit your faults to one another and pray for each other so that you may be healed" (5:16a).

Seeking support means, then, that you admit you have a problem. Most of the time, family and friends have just been waiting for this opportunity. They want to help if only you will give them a chance.

Other values also come out of seeking their support. Revealing your problem to them gives you added incentive to change. You simply don't want to have to go back to them and admit you've failed. On one occasion, I realized the need to break a bad habit that had given me problems for years. The habit was somewhat embarrassing, so I had carefully concealed it from everyone. When the time came to break it, I went to a close friend, told him about it, and asked for his prayerful support. I told him that I thought I was to the point where if I just knew that someone else was aware of my problem, I could lick it. That was all I needed. Once I told someone else about my problem, it disappeared. The prospect of having to go back and admit failure gave me sufficient motivation.

On the other hand, you will also need the support that comes when people no longer pressure you to engage in your habit. Family and friends, remember, are also major sources of temptation. If they will only give you their active support by *not* tempting you, it will mean a great deal. It will diminish the pressures you have to face and make success easier.

All of this relates to a verse in the book of Ecclesiastes:

> Two can accomplish more than twice a much as one, for the results can be much better. If one falls, the other pulls him up; but if a man falls when he is alone, he's in trouble. Also, on a cold night, two under the same blanket

gain warmth from each other, but how can one be warm alone? And one standing alone can be attacked and defeated, but two can stand back-to-back and conquer; three is even better, for a triple-braided cord is not easily broken. (4:9-12)

In saying this, Solomon was telling us that if we will only join with others in our battles, we will increase our chances of succeeding (which is why this book works best as part of a class in which people support one another's efforts to change).

Who should help you? What family? What friends?

First, the best helpers are those who see you regularly. If you write your parents or brothers and sisters and they live a thousand miles away, they won't really be much help except for their prayer support, valuable though that may be. You need someone who can see you regularly, who sees you engage in your habit and can remind you of your plan. This means people from your home, your work, and wherever else you go with any degree of regularity. (When dealing with sexual habits, the person is a checkpoint rather than an actual observer.)

These should also be people from whom you can accept criticism without getting upset. There are always people who would gladly help you because they love every opportunity they can get to cut somebody down. That sort of help you don't need. Can you imagine Paul asking his Jewish opponents for help in breaking a habit? In fact, if you choose someone who enjoys seeing your weakness, you will probably rebel and fall into your habit just to spite them. Choose people you respect and whose criticism you can accept without getting angry.

When I'm counseling a person about a habit, the first question I usually ask is, "Could we ask your spouse to help us with this habit?" Many people give a weak smile and comment, "I'd really rather we looked for someone else." What they realize is that if their spouse were pointing out their failures, they'd fail just for the sake of getting back. Or, on the other hand, they know their spouse would attack rather than help, and they don't want that type of feedback.

How do you approach a family member or friend seeking help?

Go to them and explain just what it is you want. Tell them you want them to remind you every time they see you engaging in your habit, because you often aren't aware of what you are doing. At the same time, explain why you want their help. You value their assistance, and you need the incentive that comes from knowing they are supporting you. Rightly done, you are telling them that you honor them.

At the same time, you want to tell them to be gentle in their criticisms. Most of us are sensitive about our failures. If when you fail someone jumps on your back with hobnail boots, you are going to be crushed. They need to remind you gently of your plan.

They also should not jump on you as soon as they notice what you are doing. Your goal is self-discipline. If someone else is jumping on you the moment you do something wrong, you won't develop self-discipline. Ask them to give you a few moments to react yourself. Then, if you don't respond, they should speak with you. (Sometimes speaking is not appropriate, so a prearranged signal will work.

Phyllis does this with me. When I'm speaking, I tend to become so involved in what I'm doing that I scowl, giving people the impression I'm unhappy. Phyllis saw this and volunteered to help me break the habit. But since I'm speaking in public, she can't say anything. Instead she just looks at me, frowns herself, and puts her finger on her nose pointing to the scowl. The moment I see her, I know what I'm doing wrong and change.

When people bring your habit to your attention, be appreciative. Thank them for what they have done, and let them know that you appreciate their continued help. (When Phyllis points out my scowl, I smile at her to say thanks.) If you react negatively, they will soon realize you don't really want their help. Then they will say nothing and you won't have the support you need.

I learned that lesson through a bad experience. When I was a college student, I was hypercritical of everything going on around me. Most of my conversations were criticisms of other people. During my junior year, I realized this was a problem and asked some friends for help. A few days later as we sat eating lunch, Jon commented, "Chuck, you're being awfully critical. You asked me to remind you when I heard you. Well,

I'm reminding you." I gave him a dirty look, but I stopped. However, he never brought up the subject again. My response stifled any further desire he might have had to help me.

You should also report your progress to your helpers at specified intervals. This encourages them to keep helping while it builds incentive for you to improve between reporting periods so that you do not face the embarrassment of having to report less success than last time. This brings us back to the value of a progress chart. If you keep a progress chart, it encourages you and also provides a concrete basis for a status report each time you talk with them.

Finally, display your improvement without overdoing it. Talk with others about your progress. Don't talk so exclusively about your progress, however, that you become a bore. There is nothing quite so dull as a person who is successfully breaking a bad habit and can talk of nothing else. You can also display your improvement in other ways. New clothing can accent the change resulting from your weight loss. You can lay your hands out on the table as you sit with others so they can see your nice new nails. You can let people see the present you bought for your wife with the money you saved since you stopped smoking. Without being a bore, seek opportunities to let your friends know how well you are succeeding.

When should you contact those who are going to help you? Before you start your attempt to break your habit. Let them know when you plan to begin, and enlist their support for that time.

Problems

So far we have focused on the help family and friends can give. Few people can do as much to help as they can. But on the other hand, few people can do as much to subvert your plans. Without even working at it, they can sabotage your most careful strategies. In fact, recent studies of relapse among people attempting to break a habit have shown that the factor most often involved in relapses is social pressure. It outweighs all others in significance. So we need to look closely at this problem.

Family and friends are sources of temptation. As I read

the story of the first sin in Genesis 3, I'm impressed with the role social pressure played. After Eve sinned, she offered the fruit to Adam. He in turn ate it. Eve could claim that she had been deceived by Satan. And she had been, even if she did enjoy the deception because it permitted her to do what she wanted to do anyhow. But Adam could not claim to have been deceived. He ate with his eyes wide open. What he could claim was pressure from his wife. But did she really pressure him? Not if we think of pressure as her nagging him until he gave in. What, then, was the pressure? The simple offer made by someone Adam loved. Few pressures are greater than an offer to sin made by someone you love.

Through social pressure, family and friends encourage bad habits as a means of relieving stress and boredom. Probably the most obvious relate to four of our more common failings. When you are nervous or bored, society recommends that you have a cocktail, smoke a cigarette, get something to eat, or go out and buy something. Yet these common means of relieving stress and boredom contribute to habits that are some of the most difficult to break. This means, then, that you need to face these pressures and deal with them.

In some instances, this will mean redefining relationships with others. JoAnn and Shirley, sisters, have stayed single beyond the age when most women marry. Even though they have separate apartments, they spend a great deal of time with one another. Over the years, they have fallen into the habit of eating almost any time they get together.

For the past month, JoAnn has been attempting to maintain a regular calorie intake of 1200 daily. She succeeds most of the time. But any time Shirley is around, she fails.

As JoAnn began to analyze her failures, she found it necessary to sit down and talk with Shirley. She explained the changes she wanted to make and made it plain that she expected Shirley to cooperate. While Shirley didn't particularly like the change, she agreed because of her love for her sister. In a later conversation, JoAnn admitted that her talk with Shirley was one of the hardest things she ever did.

With more serious problems, it may even be necessary to sever a relationship. Many successful programs dealing with drug and alcohol addiction encourage people to seek new friends. When friendships destroy a person's resolve to break a habit and the habit is a serious one, those friendships have to be broken.

On an even deeper level, I was once involved in counseling a man whose oldest son was introducing his younger brothers and sisters to drugs. We worked for a while with the problem, but we eventually saw that we simply could not control the older boy's behavior. At that point, the father asked his son to leave and stay away from home until his drug problems were resolved or his brothers and sisters were grown up. It broke the father's heart, but he knew it had to be.

Family and friends may cause problems because they do not like you to change. That may sound strange. Why should family and friends not want you to break a habit? The reason is that they are accustomed to living with you as you are. (We might say that they are habituated to your behavior.) If you change, they will have to change. Since most people don't like to change, they will resist, consciously or unconsciously, your attempts to change.

Your changing might also make them uncomfortable, because it may point out areas in which they need to change. Your change implies criticism of their lifestyle, even though you don't intend it. It may make them jealous of your will power. It may make them feel badly about themselves. When these things happen, the simplest thing for them to do is prevent you from changing. Then they will feel better. You need to be aware of this so that you will not be surprised by their resistance.

We also need to recognize that being with others who share our habit makes change difficult. The smell of cigarette smoke creates problems for the person who is trying to stop smoking. The smell of alcohol creates a renewed desire in the person who is trying to stop drinking. The smell of food almost causes stomach cramps for some people who are trying to lose weight. While you cannot entirely avoid these situations, you have to recognize the ones that cause problems for you and either avoid them or steel yourself ahead of time to resist the temptation. Here again, the power of the Holy Spirit can be crucial — He can supply the discipline you might not have in and of yourself.

Part of the social pressure we face comes from feelings we have about what is right. Christians often feel they do not have the rights others have, but you do have certain rights relative to the expectations of others, and I don't think you can break a bad habit unless you live by them. For example, you have the right to judge what is best for you and to be responsible for the consequences. You have the right to act without defending or justifying your actions to anyone but God so long as you are satisfied you are doing His will. You have the right *not* to conform to others' expectations for you. You have the right to be wrong — and to suffer the consequences. You have the right to change your mind. You have the right to your opinions, desires, and feelings. Unless you believe these things to be true, you will have a hard time resisting social pressure.

Because social pressure can be such a big problem, you should plan ahead of time how you're going to resist it. I would even suggest that you write out what you would do in some of the more common situations you face.

A key element of this is teaching yourself how to say no graciously. Most people fail in the face of social pressure because they haven't learned this simple social grace. Saying no kindly means you first of all thank the person who makes you an offer. Second, say no without making an elaborate statement of your reasons or defense of what you're doing. That generally just embarrasses the other person. Third, whenever possible, give the other person an alternative that you would enjoy so that you take him off the spot.

Here's how I handle it when the work I do involves me with people who drink, which I don't. Over the years I've learned to respond to an offer of a glass of wine with "Thanks for the offer, but I'd really rather not. But if you have a glass of pop or fruit juice, I would appreciate that." This acknowledges their concern in making the offer, but at the same time it makes plain my refusal. I also immediately give them an alternative that lets them graciously do something else.

Another means of overcoming social pressure is advance notice. June has been struggling for some time with her drinking problem, but her job involves regular cocktail parties. At last she hit on a solution that works for her. Before she goes to a cocktail party, she calls the hostess on the phone and explains that she cannot drink. At the same time, she asks if the hostess can supply her with a fruit punch or soda in a cocktail glass for the evening. She drinks little or nothing from the glass, thus keeping people from offering to get her a cocktail. She also gives the appearance of fitting in, even though she does not drink. Many times you can avoid difficult situations by talking to the people involved before the situation becomes difficult.

But this takes practice, so you need to work at it. You can do that by writing out how you expect to handle difficult situations. You can also do it just in your imagination. The best way to do it, however, is to act it out with a friend playing the role of the person making the offer. During your practice, anticipate various reactions from others — embarrassment, continued pressure, pressure to the point of being offensive. Plan how you would respond to each situation. In this way you will arm yourself ahead of time for each encounter.

However, you are not going to succeed every time. Occasionally you are going to fail. When that happens, it's important that you look realistically at your failures, discover why you failed, and establish a plan to avoid failure in the future. More about that in the next chapter.

Assignment:

1. Seek a friend to support you as you try to change.
2. With a friend, role play resisting common temptations you face. Particularly learn how to say no graciously.

Further reading:

Charles Cerling, *Assertiveness and the Christian* (Tyndale).

14

Recovering from Failure

You're just about ready to begin breaking your bad habit. But before you begin, you need a warning. You're going to fail. That's right. You're going to fail. I'm warning you ahead of time so that you will take failure in stride. I'm not saying you'll fail completely. I'm saying you'll not succeed *every* time you face a new temptation. So expect some failures in your attempt to break your habit.

In fact, welcome your failures as teachers that reveal weak points in your plan so you can strengthen them. In preparation for his debate with Jimmy Carter in the 1980 presidential race, Ronald Reagan enlisted David Stockman to play devil's advocate. Stockman studied Carter's speeches and ideas until he felt he could represent Carter in a debate with Reagan. He then did his best to shoot holes in Reagan's arguments as a means of preparing him to debate Carter. Similarly, each failure is a new teacher, trying to show you how you can more effectively defeat subsequent temptations.

In any new project, your initial efforts will include some failures. You need a time of learning. Learning means you will occasionally fail as you proceed along the path toward acquiring a new form of behavior. You do not want your failures, however, to go to waste. So you analyze each one to determine how to win the next round. You return to the chart in chapter 7 to examine the items surrounding your failures. What events, people, attitudes, thoughts, emotions, and time contributed to your failure? By looking closely at these things, you will gain an even better picture of your habit than you had before. Now you can use this new information to strengthen your plan and improve your chances for success — for greater freedom to minister — in the future.

Let's examine briefly two areas where potential failures seem to cluster. First, most failures grow out of social pressure. There is nothing quite like an invitation from a friend to destroy your motivation to change. Thus, you need to be particularly aware of this area of weakness. Teen Challenge, in its highly acclaimed program for taking people off drugs, realizes the problems related to social pressure. As a result, it removes people from their home environment and takes them to a farm, where they stay until they have broken the habit. The key element of treatment is getting them away from social pressure. Even if you can't afford to leave where you are, you can make plans to counter social pressure based on the preceding chapter.

Frustration and anger often team up with social pressure to defeat the person trying to break a habit. In fact, frustration and anger in association with social pressure account for more failures than all other causes combined. So you need to be particularly watchful of those situations where these elements team up on you. Suppose, for example, that you're upset and frustrated because of unfair treatment at work, but you're trying to quit smoking — and you're going to a party tonight at which you know almost everyone will be smoking. You particularly need to fortify yourself at such times. By thinking them through ahead of time and planning what you will do as suggested in the last chapter, you can win.

A destructive philosophy of change destroys other people's plans to change. This philosophy says you're either a success or a failure. It leaves no room for middle ground. This philosophy is wrong.

When you attempt to break a habit, you will move from few successes to more successes. You will move from many failures to fewer failures. Any attempt to change involves moving from little or no success and many failures to increasing levels of success with fewer failures.

We have become trapped in the philosophy that God either completely frees a person from a habit immediately or He does nothing at all. The all-or-nothing philosophy, however, is a device of the devil to keep you from continuing after you have failed. You need to remember that most of baseball's greatest home run hitters, such as Babe Ruth, have also been leaders in strikeouts. The person who plans to succeed needs to have the initiative to keep going even in the face of failure.

Closely related to this idea is the idea that you must not give up too early. As noted before, doctors are constantly frustrated with patients who quit taking their medicine as soon as obvious symptoms of the disease are gone. Counselors see a similar phenomenon among their clients. People come suffering from psychological distress. As the counselor begins to work with them, their distress diminishes. Then they quit coming to counseling, even though the counselor knows they have not conquered their problem. They quit too soon, and he knows he will be seeing them again because they have not killed all the psychological bacteria. So don't quit until you have lived free of symptoms for at least a month. Only by doing this will you assure yourself of victory.

You also need to remember the nature of habits and change. Habits persist because they are easy. We don't change because change is hard. It means work, and habits cater to our natural laziness. Thus we tend to resist change. This means you need to concentrate on working at overcoming your habits.

You also need to remember the signs of change. Evidence of change is indicated when you experience temptations less frequently than you have in the past, when your temptations are less intense than they have been, or when your temptations grow shorter in duration. If any of these indicators change, you are succeeding. You cannot expect complete success in one day. You should anticipate a struggle that you will win, but the war is not going to be finished in a night.

Recovering from failure means dealing with guilt after you have fallen. I have already said that failing is a natural part of learning how to do something new. But when the failing involves sin, guilt is also a part of learning to do something new. How should you handle that? First, you should not focus on your failure and guilt, but on your successes. You should congratulate yourself on the times when you have succeeded.

But you also cannot dismiss or overlook your guilt. You need to deal with it. Why do you think God said through John, "But if we confess our sins to Him, He can be depended on to forgive us and to cleanse us from every wrong" (1 John 1:9)?

God knew we needed the provision He makes for our forgiveness in that verse. If He had expected us to succeed every time we tried to break a bad habit, we would not need forgiveness. God's telling us He will forgive us when we confess our sins suggests that He anticipates our failures. Thus, He knows we will fail and He makes provision for our forgiveness so that we can put our failures behind us and move on toward victory by confessing our sin and asking the Holy Spirit to fill us again.

This means, then, that you can rest in God's love even when you fail. Only a loving heavenly Father could make such provision *ahead of time*. Knowing you would fail and need forgiveness, He made provision ahead of time. That is love! Because God loves you, you are free to try — and even to fail while trying.

I learned this as a staff member in a large church. I had lived with the constant fear of failure in some of the churches I served earlier in my life, but not there. The senior minister, Don, gave me the freedom to try and fail. When I failed, he never complained. He just asked what I thought I could do next time to prevent the same thing from happening. I appreciated that. He gave me the freedom to fail, because he knew that without the freedom to fail, I didn't have the freedom to try anything new.

Now we come to the hard part. You might try and not succeed. You might have underlying problems that are sufficiently serious that you can't break your habit yourself. You might need professional help. What indicates this? A couple of things. If you begin work on your habit and find that you make no progress even though you do everything suggested in this book, you might need help from a professional counselor. Or if you try to break a habit and make progress but never quite succeed in freeing yourself from the habit, you may need to seek a counselor.

How long should you try? That depends on the habit you're trying to break. Habits like knuckle cracking, fingernail biting, and other surface habits should yield rather quickly to the method we suggest. Habits like alcoholism, drug addiction, and smoking will probably take longer. In the instances of simpler items, if the habit is not gone in a month, something is probably wrong. With the more serious habits, it might take you a year of work before you see the need for counseling. We can never overlook the fact, however, that you might need more help than this book can give. If so, seek a professional counselor to help you break your habit.

15

The Beginning

Now what? If you have done as I suggested in the first chapter, you are ready to begin. You read the book through to get the big picture. You know what to do. Now go through the book again, step by step, and follow the procedure outlined. Each step is important. Don't rush through them or you'll guarantee your complete failure. Unless you're a very unusual person, you did not get enough information the first time through to break your habit. So return to the first chapter and begin to work your way through the book. But this time work on each project rather than just read about them.